Tumbling Stones

Tumbling Stones

12 Ideas to Develop Spiritual Grit in Families

by

Colleen O'Steen

with Haley O'Steen, Rosalind O'Steen Fort, and Claire O'Steen

Edited by Shirley Cook

Wood Family Press
Huntsville

ISBN: 978-1-7351060-0-7 (paperback)

Cover photography by Wally O'Steen
Cover design by Panciera Design

CONTENTS

FOREWORD

It is a frightening time to be a parent. From kids consumed with social media to sexual temptation and teen pregnancy to the epidemic of mass shootings at schools, there is a lot to alarm parents. But disciples have deeper concerns. We certainly want our kids to avoid the moral failures that are common among the youth in our culture. But we also want our kids to embrace faith and passionately serve Jesus. And yet we are confronted with a disturbing epidemic of young disciples who are making the inexplicable choice to abandon faith. Even more hang onto a religious facade but wallow in spiritual mediocrity.

In times like these, we need good news. We need to be reminded that our kids are not unavoidably destined to follow the path of a corrupt culture. We need to know that it is possible to raise devoted disciples even in the face of an evil world. And we need to know *how* to do this. We need to be able to take the guidance supplied in scripture and plug in day by day to the conversations and decisions made at our house.

Tumbling Stones helps us do this. The authors build on a rock-solid foundation by constantly bringing readers back to scripture. Working from this foundation, the book blends scripture with principles, illustrations, and practical strategies that help parents move easily from theory to practice. We are never left wondering how to use the ideas that the book recommends.

Tumbling Stones has a unique place among the tens of thousands of volumes written about parenting. The contributions of the author, a mother (Colleen), and her three daughters (Haley, Rosalind, and Claire) offer the reader a multigenerational view of the subject. Readers are able to see each challenge or strategy from both the parent's and child's perspectives. Also, because all four contributors are now adults, this work looks at parenting from the back side of the process. The counsel offered is time-tested.

Tumbling Stones gives us a fresh look at a subject that has been discussed for thousands of years. It is sure to give frightened parents consolation and direction as they undertake one of life's most important tasks, to bring up their children in the discipline and instruction of the Lord.

David and
Heidi Banning

INTRODUCTION

Tumbling Stones is about a process that starts with grit and ends with grit. It's about rearing children to be spiritually strong, persevering, and even strategic. Hobbyists who polish stones begin with a pile of raw material—natural stones right out of the ground. They begin to process the stones with certainty of the brilliant metamorphosis to come. They mix together the stones, the grit, and other elements. Then they start the action.

Polishing stones is a metaphor for the development of children under the gritty guidance of parents, grandparents, teachers, and other leaders. They persevere to create a remarkable and gleaming result that retains the grit, unlike the polished stones, which are rinsed of theirs in the end. Yes, we want our kids to keep the grit.

Transforming and improving something is always an exhilarating endeavor, especially through the hopes of youth. When I was a child, I had a little apparatus that tumbled stones to polish them. The picture on the box showed everyday rocks changing into sparkling gems, and boy, was I excited. I put rough stones into the plastic canister, added coarse grit and water, and screwed on the lid. Then I placed the container on its side on top of the machine that rotated it perpetually. I wanted to peek but waited a week to open it. When I looked inside, it was a sloppy, anticlimactic mess.

I poured out the slop and rinsed the rocks with water to eliminate every speck of mud and grit. Then I inspected. If any stones were ill-shaped or not refined enough, you were supposed to put them back through step one for another week.

Every seven days I poured out the muddy stones, rinsed them, and repeated the tumbling process, using a finer grit with each step. After about one month, my rough stones had been polished to a brilliant, colorful state. They looked like diamonds and rubies to me, even though they were just common stones benefiting from tender, exacting care.

It's a nice analogy for burnishing our children to bring out their true potential, their luster. This extensive process is much more untidy than we could imagine. As with the rough rocks, we look at that willful toddler and are able to envision something of socially redeeming value years down the road. With children, we get into the tumbler with them, and we hope the grit stays with them long after, bringing strength when it needs to.

The stones roll and jostle up against other stones that have various impacts and actions, just like the people a child encounters. The grinding and water have their effect on our precious stones, just like conversations, the laws of nature, events, and physical development influence a child.

In the Bible stones are a foundation, as when Jesus is described using an architectural metaphor for the spiritual house's foundational cornerstone: "chosen by God and precious" (1 Peter 2:4). Stones mean something indestructible that carries on the ideals of mortals, as when the Israelites commemorate their crossing into the promised land with twelve stones representing the sons of Jacob (see Joshua 4). Christians, elevated to a new worth "as living stones, are being built up a spiritual house, a holy priesthood, to offer up spiritual sacrifices acceptable to God through Jesus Christ" (1 Peter 2:5). If we are living stones, then our kids are living stones in the making, with the ability to carry on their own faith in God after we are gone.

This book is a team writing effort and includes the viewpoints of me (Colleen), a mom who is of the baby boom generation, and my daughters, Haley, Rosalind, and Claire, all of the millennial generation. In writing such a book, our first inclination was to recoil from championing particular strategies for teaching moral uprightness, for fear of appearing self-righteous and bragging of quick answers to complicated questions. We felt the recoil, withstood it, and decided to get everything out in the open at the beginning.

We haven't cornered the wisdom market, but we do have experience to share. We don't execute perfectly, and it's unseen how our lives and decisions will unfold in the future, but here's what we agree on: We care deeply about our fellow Christians and their children who will follow. We care so much that we're willing to let our masks slip a little to share life experiences and the strategies we've used to reinforce our souls.

We're willing to lay down our cards and reveal what worked, what didn't, and what we think will bring success in the future. Ours is a tiny start, a gift to set you a step ahead and help you give your personal talent and devotion to God so that the term "grit" will work a great strength in your family tree. It may even move you to the next level and to a more profound and brimming storehouse of God's blessings, never before entertained because you can't experience the next level until you arrive. Grit won't carry you; it will drive you there.

1

SOFT LIFE, LITTLE GRIT: WHO HAS GRIT, AND WHERE CAN WE GET SOME?

Colleen

We were enjoying a wholesome American summer day at the Madison County Beekeepers picnic in Huntsville, Alabama. On the periphery of the scene of deviled eggs, picnic tables, and crowded conversation, there was a bright green dab, out of place and not man-made, at eye level on a tree. I was curious. Upon investigating I saw it was a cicada, alive on arrival, struggling to be born and squeezing into the world from its drab, brittle shell.

I called my three young daughters, Haley, Rosalind, and Claire, to come quick and watch the natural marvel. We studied the juicy process as the chartreuse newborn nearly imperceptibly overpowered the shell that had been its home. After about fifteen minutes, the labor was complete, and the healthy cicada with two bulging eyes clung to the tree, resting in peace as we gawked dotingly at our little newborn baby bug.

"No!" In an instant an attacker swept in for the strike. By reflex we swung and flapped at the assaulting force, not realizing at first what it was. It was a cicada killer wasp. What we were cooing over it had been salivating for from a covert position. In vain we shooed and yelled as the wasp, in no way daunted by our protests, continued to sting the cicada.

It would be clever and graceful to finish this story with some obscure fact about the cicada's gaining vitality by fighting the wasp stings and to say that it went on to live its natural cicada life cycle—but that's not the plot here. Most likely, the cicada was paralyzed with the first sting and rendered fresh food for the wasp, which does make it a great analogy for the heartless realities of this world and the way we make our way with God relative to the world's outside forces.

Our own young, newly introduced to the world, are potential food for the wasps unless we infuse in them strategies for defending and charging ahead no matter what. We must give them not just information but a practical and trustworthy game plan. This has little to do with flapping away the wasps and everything to do with building hearts and minds that are two steps ahead, two stratagems out. It's grit; that's the heart of the matter.

Jesus says not to worry about comfort in this world (Matthew 6:25) or about dying (Hebrews 2:14–15). He says to "Be faithful until death" (Revelation 2:10). These verses are easy to read yet improbable to practice. One key characteristic of those who can follow through is grit—that is, unbeatable spirit, pluck, unflagging determination in the face of deprivation and tribulation. Like money in a retirement account, grit is not something we summon for the first time the day we really need it. It is developed over decades and often against our will, because in many ways, staying power is the product of adversity. We still want our kids to have it, even though life may be soft now. And once they have it, we want them to use it every time, in every way, from dawn to dusk, no matter what it takes.

"Gritty" is how people describe those who hang on, stay tough, and stand firm through ill fortune, sickness, or any number of troubles brought on by other people. It's not until you run the gauntlet that you are described as having grit. It's something you develop, something you own, a thing you use as a weapon and a shield. You can't buy it, but you can earn it—that's how you pay for it. Pay for it with pain, suffering, tears, shame, anger, disappointment, and loss. We want it for ourselves and also for our children, but we do not line up happily to foot the bill and certainly are not prodding our kids forward to pay the price. How can we rear our young ones with spiritual tenacity when life in our time is light on the ordeals that form it? In our civilization of low infant mortality rates, longer life spans, peace, and plentiful consumer goods, how can we build this grit quality in children, grandchildren, and students when many naturally have easy lives, few tears, and little true pain? To begin to answer the question, consider examples of this fortitude in the Bible.

Grit or Not in the Scriptures

In the Bible the values of endurance and tenacity are woven into the narrative from beginning to end. Bible characters may lack grit, have grit and use it, or possess it and not use it. Scripture leaves no doubt that it is favorable in God's sight to endure in faithfulness to Him. Two biblical characters, in particular, exemplify resolution that follows through or courage that crumbles in the crunch.

Rahab the harlot (see Joshua 2 and 6) establishes herself as an unlikely hero when she saves Joshua's spies in Jericho and helps Israel to achieve its first victory after crossing into Canaan. Yes, she is a harlot; yes, she tells a bald-faced lie. However, she is just beginning to understand who the true, living God is. Her initial faith is built on fear and awe at the stories of God's feats, and she is most likely ignorant of the Law of Moses. The Bible does not condone this questionable evidence about Rahab but states it as fact.

It's also a fact that this woman is impressive when it comes to strategy and knowing how to work a deal. She perceives that the spies are on the winning side and shows no hesitation to craft a plan for their safety and escape. Even when it means defying the king of Jericho and risking her life, Rahab hides the spies on her roof and sends their pursuers off on a wild goose chase to buy a little time. Before she says goodbye to the spies, there's a pact to be pledged, and she doesn't shrink from defining the terms: her silence in return for her family's salvation when Israel attacks.

The promises are sealed with a red cord and clinched with Rahab's final instructions for the spies to hide in the mountains three days and then go home. The spies follow her strategy to a T and make it back to Joshua with the news. It appears that Rahab has at least two weeks—perhaps waiting on tenterhooks—to rethink her allegiance while Israel makes its way toward and then circles Jericho, a sitting duck.

When the dust settles, Rahab and her family are faithfully waiting behind the red cord in the window. She goes on to be held up by James as an example of faith undergirded by works: "You see then that a man is justified by works, and not by faith only. Likewise, was not Rahab the harlot also justified by works when she received the messengers and sent them out another way?" (James 2:24–25). Rahab has nerve and a strategic mind to prove her faith. So does the apostle Peter—sometimes.

Peter can be remembered as an example of great boldness for Christ, a man who is beaten and imprisoned for his faith but preaches anyway. Peter is also one whose determination can crumble in the crunch. I can't explain this inconsistency, but I draw conclusions from it.

After having the fearlessness to accuse the Pentecost crowd of crucifying the Son of God (Acts 2:36) and after converting the first gentile, Cornelius (Acts 10), Peter then yields to peer pressure, as described by the apostle Paul:

> Now when Peter had come to Antioch, I withstood him to his face, because he was to be blamed; for before certain men came from James, he would eat with the Gentiles; but when they came, he withdrew and separated himself, fearing those who were of the circumcision. (Galatians 2:11–12)

Prejudice and hypocrisy can come in subtle forms, which makes them scary. They don't feel that wrong sometimes. Unlike Rahab under pressure, Peter's life is not threatened; he is just uncomfortable socially. He appears to have been merely unwilling to take a stand for what the Holy Spirit had established concerning the cleansed state of the gentiles. This was illustrated to Peter in a vision in Joppa (Acts 10:15) and to the apostles in Jerusalem when they debated the issue of circumcision for gentile Christians (Acts 15). The application of this teaching is that Jews and gentiles should now mix as one in Christ. Peter knows it but then ignores it under cultural tension.

That's when we know whether we have that unbreakable spiritual toughness—in the crunch. Peter and other Jews mingle and eat with the gentile Christians, having embraced the new relationship admirably. The moment of truth comes when more Jews arrive, and he distances himself from the gentiles.

We can all identify with Peter's weakness. So how can we develop our children—and ourselves—to be analytical and able to self-indict in such situations? How can we possess the unfailing fortitude of Rahab and her unbroken spirit at the crucial point? Her ability to see past the present distress?

If Rahab had approached Jesus asking what she should do to inherit eternal life—yes, I know she was His direct ancestor, but indulge me—when He told her to sell all her belongings, give to the poor, and follow Him, would she have complied or walked away? Given that precise situation, the rich young ruler leaves, because his estate is extensive and divestiture to benefit the penniless is too much to ask (Matthew 19:16–22). Based on the little revealed about her in the scriptures, I guess that Rahab would have sold everything and fallen in with Jesus's flock.

We know a little more about what Peter would have done if in the rich young ruler's shoes. After observing Jesus's exchange with the rich young ruler and the teaching that it is difficult for a rich man to enter heaven, Peter declares, "We have left all and followed You" (Matthew 19:27). Now we can add that to Peter's list of meritorious deeds: leaving his worldly goods behind.

This is key to the conversation about spiritual pluck, because Peter definitely has it—except when he doesn't. Me too. This inconsistency thickens the plot for igniting the next generation to stand firm. It is not enough to resist in the throes of persecution only sometimes, not enough to stand fearlessly with Christ only occasionally, as when Peter takes up the sword at Jesus's arrest (John 18:10).

You and I are never past being tested either. You would think that one who preaches despite physical danger would have this tenacity thing all sewn up. If Peter could withstand death threats, he could endure peer pressure, right? No. In fact Peter seems particularly vulnerable in this area, as when he—even cursing and swearing—denies Christ, claiming, "I do not know this Man of whom you speak!" (Mark 14:71). What compels him to reject Jesus three times (Matthew 26:69–75), when Peter had just declared that would never happen? It is Peter's intense aversion to being seen as unacceptable by others.

Standing around a fire, warming himself during Jesus's trial, Peter is not physically threatened. His companions are merely stating the connection between him and Jesus, yet he lies to dissociate himself from his teacher, his Lord. Therefore, it is not out of the question that we might stand firm in the most rigorous of moral battles yet botch mightily the relatively simple challenges.

But there's hope. We and those growing up now can defeat this exasperating irregularity by knowing ourselves. This means being able to self-analyze so that we plan for our strong points, our weak ones, and the pitfalls we haven't yet encountered.

Now, consider examples from the twentieth century and beyond. We will here draw conclusions about two people who prevailed even though they endured troublesome circumstances from childhood.

A Girl's Hardship and Victorious Faith

Carrie Johnson lay on her bed in the late afternoon of August 9, 1996, listening to recorded hymns. She suffered a stroke that evening and passed away the next day at age eighty-nine, according to her daughter, Shirley Cook, who related this story. Carrie had been a happy woman living a rewarding Christian life. She made friends wherever she lived and was lovingly called "Grandma" by the Christians around her. She served God faithfully, living with her daughter and preacher son-in-law and accompanying him on his evangelistic and benevolent visits. She fed the hungry, cared for the sick, and loved God and people. Those at Carrie's funeral would have described her this way, but they didn't see her childhood and young adult years. If they had, they would have made the correlation between the adversity she experienced at the beginning of her life and her perseverance later on.

Born on a tobacco farm in Kentucky in 1907, Carrie was the oldest child in her family. Five more children were born and survived, bringing the count to eight people living in a two-room dwelling. Since her mother was frequently pregnant and sick, Carrie reared her siblings, grew food in the garden and canned it, cooked, and helped to harvest tobacco. She rose at dawn to feed chickens, gather eggs, milk cows by hand, slop hogs, and cook breakfast on a wood-fired stove. By hand she drew water for washing dishes and doing laundry—this laundry including a steady stream of dirty cloth diapers. Then it was time for lunch, and if workers were helping in the field, she served extra food at the table.

Carrie's family worshipped with the Lynnville church of Christ. She became a Christian around age fourteen. Approximately two years later, Carrie's mother died of pneumonia shortly after giving birth to her last child.

It's difficult to imagine how under the tremendous responsibility she bore, but Carrie gained an education through the sixth grade. By age eighteen, Carrie was married to Jack Johnson, and the two moved to Akron, Ohio. At age nineteen, Carrie gave birth to a baby girl who was born with a severe heart defect. When Jackieleen died at nine months of age, the two heartbroken parents took the body back to Kentucky to bury and then returned to Akron. These were dark days for the couple, with no family and few friends nearby. They had never associated themselves with a congregation of God's people in Akron.

Then things started looking up, and in 1929 a healthy baby girl was born to Carrie and Jack. Securing a job as a letter carrier with the US Postal Service, Jack had a regular paycheck during the Great Depression. However, more trouble awaited the young family. You wouldn't think the duties of a mailman a source of moral temptation, but they were. Jack's mail route included small businesses, such as grocery stores and bars. Delivering mail to these on a daily basis exposed him to the availability of alcohol, and he gave in to the desire to drink.

The couple was able to buy a house, and Carrie gave birth to another healthy baby girl in 1935. It is here that we begin to see childhood adversity manifest itself in Carrie as she determined to renew her commitment to God and began attending worship services of the Thayer Street Church of Christ in Akron. She would be faithful for the rest of her life, but it took tenacity.

Jack refused to drive Carrie and the girls—then ages ten and four—to church services. Carrie never learned to drive, so the three traveled by city bus. This involved walking several blocks to the bus stop (with Ohio winter temperatures near zero degrees), riding downtown, transferring to another bus, and walking from the Thayer Street stop to the church building. It was a one-hour commute each way.

After the bombing of Pearl Harbor, Jack took on a factory shift in addition to his postal job. He began to absent himself from home, sometimes overnight and even for multiple days. The drinking worsened. This cocky young man became a belligerent tyrant, physically and verbally abusing Carrie and the children. Sending the girls to the neighbor's house when he was on a rampage, Carrie did her best to maintain the marriage and their home life.

These both came to an end when Jack walked out on his family and began openly living with another woman. Carrie and Jack were divorced in 1944. It began a new phase in Carrie's life that required patience, faith, and a whole lot of fortitude.

Carrie had full custody of the girls, by that time ages fifteen and nine. She also got the house. Jack was ordered by law to pay child support but didn't. It must have taken a very strong will for Carrie to refuse to take Jack to court for the unpaid funds. Instead she worked like a dog just to subsist. Her daughters started jobs as teenagers, helping to pay for utilities and upkeep on the house, not to mention paying for daily food and other necessities.

Carrie was blessed with good health and a strong spirit, owing in part, no doubt, to a life of hard work and striving as a child on the farm. She believed that with God's help she could do whatever was necessary to care for her children. Domestic skills were her valuable assets, so she cleaned other people's houses, did laundry, and took care of children. After a hard day's work, she spent most evenings ironing men's shirts for customers who paid ten cents each.

It wasn't just work ethic that paid her bills, though. She also was strategic and figured out how to make deals with people. For instance, one of her neighbors had a grocery store. Carrie would buy necessary food, charge it, and then clean the store owner's house as often as needed to pay the bill. At one time during World War II, Carrie and the girls shared one bedroom in their house and rented the other bedroom to a war bride and her little girl. In addition to the rent, Carrie was also paid to take care of the child. Through those lean years, the little family survived on bread and gravy—and an occasional treat of grilled cheese sandwiches (Cook 2018).

Like the innocent baby cicada attacked by the killer wasp, Carrie was born into a life of sorrow, hard labor, and little comfort, but it conditioned her for struggles both physical and spiritual ahead. My children, husband, and I haven't encountered anything like this hardship. How would we rise to the assaults she and her family faced? How would our children pull through?

A Boy Withstands the Turbulent Sixties

When Steve Watts told his wife that he was going on a trip soon and the plans were already set, she was shocked (Watts 2018). "What trip?" According to Steve, he hadn't mentioned it to her until then because he knew she would think it an unwise decision. It was a mission trip, like others he'd made in the past, preaching the gospel of

Christ in other countries. This time he went to Panama with a group of Christians, including a number of American college students. He may have done as much in preaching to them as to the Panamanians.

He told them the story of his conversion to Christ using Romans 6:3–6 to describe the way that conversion started him in his new life, leaving behind his old life to drown in the baptismal waters:

> Or do you not know that as many of us as were baptized into Christ Jesus were baptized into His death? Therefore, we were buried with Him through baptism into death, that just as Christ was raised from the dead by the glory of the Father, even so we also should walk in newness of life. For if we have been united together in the likeness of His death, certainly we also shall be in the likeness of His resurrection, knowing this, that our old man was crucified with Him, that the body of sin might be done away with, that we should no longer be slaves of sin.

Steve had the undivided attention of his fellow missionaries when he spoke further on the subject of his own physical death and how that didn't worry him much. He urged them not to hold him up as admirable; only God knows when death will come, so why retreat?

Did I mention that Steve had been diagnosed with pancreatic cancer about one year before he went on this mission trip? He had recently completed a cycle of chemotherapy. He felt pretty good, although he suffered from fatigue and some other side effects—hence his wife's concern about his leaving the country.

When destiny threw Steve Watts a death threat, he caught it and turned it into a microphone. "More doors have been opened for me because of the word 'cancer' than I would have ever—ever—believed," he marvels. For example, Steve used Facebook to announce the cancer diagnosis to his high school classmates. He told them he wanted to have a Bible class with them before he died; it was on his "bucket" list.

Within a day or so, about forty-three had signed up for his class on authority in religion. He posted a recording of his one-hour lesson on Facebook, and at last count, more than 1,100 people had watched at least seven minutes' worth. This is far beyond what he'd expected when he invited his classmates.

This capacity to charge on in the face of trouble has its roots in Steve's childhood. His parents and three older brothers lived in public housing in Atlanta in the 1950s and 1960s. He witnessed his parents' stormy marriage, as "knock-down-drag-out" fights regularly provided the soundtrack for his growing up years. His mom and dad divorced amid financial turbulence when Steve was ten years old in 1961.

Before that things had been improving for the Watts family, as the father had gotten a good promotion at work. They could move out of public housing and into a more modern, larger, rented house. However, one day a jealous coworker lay in wait for Steve's father to cross a street outside their plant and ran him down with a car. He was out of work for the better part of a year with multiple leg fractures. With no income to support the family, debt split Steve's parents further apart until they divorced.

Steve attended eleven grammar schools in various districts. "When the rent was due, we moved," he says, explaining this unstable course. Poverty did bring industriousness, though. When there was no food in the cupboard or refrigerator—literally—Steve traipsed through the roadside ditches, picking up pop bottles to redeem for five or ten cents apiece. With his hard-earned coins, he bought pinto beans, corn meal, lard, and buttermilk. His mother was ecstatic.

This Atlanta boy also learned firsthand to disdain the bad odor of sin as he witnessed dysfunction in his family members. He saw his older brothers marry their pregnant girlfriends. He tolerated his mother's boyfriends. These situations taught him the serious nature of sexual promiscuity and the dignity and freedom it destroys. This gave him extra determination to stay sexually pure.

Steve suspects the vast clouds of secondhand smoke he breathed from his dad's chain habit compromised his lung capacity when he played sports later. He remembers his dad watching "wrastlin" on TV with one cigarette in his mouth, one forked between his fingers, and another burning in an ashtray. That stark scene of his dad's addiction to nicotine and obliviousness to excess marked Steve's conviction to abstain from such vices. I'm not sure whether or not he watches wrestling on TV, though.

While Steve would never wish his broken childhood on anyone, would he have been the man he is today if not for the poor role models and poverty that set so squarely before him more desirable ways? Would he have had the grit and the guts to be the first in his family to graduate from high school and then play football on scholarship at Harding University if not for an unstable home, growling stomach, and condescending looks from society? Would he have had the fire and the nerve to travel to Panama, preaching in spite of pancreatic cancer and its ghastly implications?

Tenacity without Hardship

From the beginning of the world, in the Garden of Eden, God has been telling people to get to work, while their brains are wired to seek ease and pleasure—not work, not sweat. Few would choose to get up at the crack of dawn to slop hogs and wash dirty diapers if there were a more comfortable way. Few would choose to scour the ditches looking for pop bottles to pay for the next meal if there were an easier option. Few would opt for religious persecution or moral temptations if they could be avoided.

Therefore, if backbreaking work, extensive trouble, and gnawing deprivation—which generate tenacity—do not exist for our children, something must be engineered to bring about an unshakable faith anyway. Can strength of purpose be taught by lecture or book? Can it be learned by observation of another person? Can it be gained with fabricated scenarios? The answer is a hearty "Yes," because if it can't, we're all sunk.

Haley

Having grit is a necessity for any person who wants to be in control of her own life, and a Christian is especially that kind of person. We are called to live lives of uprightness, strength of character, and courage; passive living does not achieve this. That's where fortitude comes in. It affords us the ability to live the way we want to live—the way God commands—without bending to the whims and agendas of the world. It gives us the will to be capable citizens of the world and soldiers of Christ.

I may be young in years, but I've lived long enough to recognize a pattern in humankind. People let others make decisions for them, and what's more disturbing, they are perfectly content to let the decision-making of others rule their lives. This apathy perpetuates because people lack the nerve to make decisions that require courage, are contrary to popular sentiment, or make us less comfortable. I know. I've been there. It was hard for me to pass on that piece of birthday cake when everyone else partook. I struggled mightily to learn to play the piano when I could have played computer games after school. There were numerous distractions when I read my Bible three times through last year. But I succeeded in each task, and in the end, I am a better person for sticking to my good intentions.

Think about the ubiquitous television. I am often at friends' houses for social time where the television is another guest that constantly interrupts. I have many peers who consider television watching a required part of their day. They would not consider leaving it off during waking hours. Regardless of the programming, they watch.

For many, someone else decides what entertains, what information goes to their brains, and when it goes there. They are exposed to mildly entertaining shows at best and unwholesome or harmful material at worst, with deceptively powerful advertising in between, subtly guiding their minds to make decisions other people or organizations want them to make. In no way are they consciously deciding that watching television is the best thing for their or others' souls.

They lack the determination to stand up and improve themselves, help others, and work for the Lord.

There are many other ways I see my peers letting people make decisions for them. It's scary to see how much influence outside forces have on them. It's even more alarming to know that when it comes down to it, these people don't have the acumen to prevent the devil from making decisions for them too. If they will aimlessly watch when cable TV tells them to, what keeps them from shirking their spiritual duties when Satan says, "Relax. You worked hard today. Spread the word when you've got more energy"? That's why it's so important to be persistent and make that a virtue in our children. Without it, the devil has control. With it, our children stand a chance of boldly facing and defusing their adversity and providing strength to others.

Rosalind

Of my peers born in the early 1990s, I can think of very few who truly grew up under difficult circumstances. Not only were trials a distant phenomenon, but so many millennials were also showered with every physical object or granted every desire. I watched, and currently watch, parents protect their children from uncomfortable situations—anything from school teachers trying to discipline to a daunting plate of leafy greens served for dinner.

I cannot say for sure, but I would guess that both Carrie and Steve were harshly disciplined by teachers and willingly ate the food given to them at every meal and were thankful for it. Compared to the true trials Carrie and Steve faced, these types of situations would not even show up on their scale of difficult circumstances. Hardship and adversity come in all varieties. The trials of my childhood do not even compare to those in the childhoods of my grandparents' generation, for example. I was born into a life of happiness, easy labor, and plentiful comfort, as were many my age and younger. That makes cultivating a life of true spiritual and physical tenacity an interesting challenge.

Near the beginning of his epistle, James states that trials should awaken a sense of happiness within us, but who naturally feels joyful when something difficult presents itself in life? I know I do not. But if we keep reading, we understand that the "testing of your faith produces patience" (James 1:3), and perseverance is something we desperately need and that our children desperately need.

I should point out that I do not have children, but my unique credential is that I am an adult who was recently a child. I hope my sisters' and my perspective is one that offers a look at the topic from a less common angle.

Parents do not have to solve every shallow issue their child faces. Get into a habit of thinking of grit-building opportunities for them. Be creative. If your child lives a cushy life, maybe a trial for him is being denied exactly what he requested for Christmas, which in turn is a lesson in living a contented life like the apostle Paul (Philippians 4:11). Perhaps your child has already had numerous unfortunate circumstances in his short life. Use each one as an opportunity to help him grow strong and point him toward Christ. May each of us use our variation of hardship to guide us on a lifepath of strength and perseverance.

Claire

I can only imagine that Carrie or Steve saw doing hard things for God as a hurdle, but not an unmanageable hurdle. They had faced and passed through many trials in their lives, proving ordeals could be overcome if they worked hard. When it comes to salvation, you are the only person who can get yourself to heaven or keep yourself from heaven. When you are a person who has had to take responsibility for yourself all of your life, accepting the message of the gospel sounds like a personal call to action.

Carrie, Steve, you, and I have had God's word to comfort and secure us when we faced challenges. One good thing about being a Christian who is really looking to see what God says is that you have the opportunity to answer specifically from the Bible when people ask religious questions. Or if you see them doing something in error and you want to illustrate the right way, you have the Bible to show them.

When we think about that determination to stay faithful no matter what, it is not just what it means to me but also in relation to other people. You have to keep propping people up to convert them and keep them strong along the way. In the case of one person I taught, I didn't let him get away with giving unsubstantiated reasons for following a particular practice. I could always bring in an example from the Bible. He was worshipping with a denomination that practiced some things from the Bible but also other things they'd come up with on their own. When we stuck with the Bible as the final word, we made more progress and became stronger.

Assignments

To start, there are two main assignments enriching the content of this book:

1. Answer and discuss with a partner the discussion questions (below and at the end of each chapter).
2. Start to memorize Luke 4:1–14. Complete the memorization over the next month. This is the exchange between Satan and Jesus in the wilderness, and there is no better verbal illustration of a profound determination than Jesus's rebuttal. To commit this to memory and be able to recite it for a partner (who follows the scripture to check your words) is a useful step in building fortitude in you and your children. Our perseverance is frequently manifested in our words.

Luke 4:1–14

Then Jesus, being filled with the Holy Spirit, returned from the Jordan and was led by the Spirit into the wilderness, being tempted for forty days by the devil. And in those days He ate nothing, and afterward, when they had ended, He was hungry.

And the devil said to Him, "If You are the Son of God, command this stone to become bread."

But Jesus answered him, saying, "It is written, 'Man shall not live by bread alone, but by every word of God.'"

Then the devil, taking Him up on a high mountain, showed Him all the kingdoms of the world in a moment of time. And the devil said to Him, "All this authority I will give You, and their glory; for this has been delivered to me, and I give it to whomever I wish. Therefore, if You will worship before me, all will be Yours."

And Jesus answered and said to him, "Get behind Me, Satan! For it is written, 'You shall worship the Lord your God, and Him only you shall serve.'"

Then he brought Him to Jerusalem, set Him on the pinnacle of the temple, and said to Him, "If You are the Son of God, throw Yourself down from here. For it is written:

'He shall give His angels charge over you,
To keep you,'
and,
'In their hands they shall bear you up,
Lest you dash your foot against a stone.'"

And Jesus answered and said to him, "It has been said, 'You shall not tempt the Lord your God.'"

Now when the devil had ended every temptation, he departed from Him until an opportune time.

Then Jesus returned in the power of the Spirit to Galilee, and news of Him went out through all the surrounding region.

Introduction and Chapter 1 Discussion Questions

1. How do you see the analogy of polishing stones in relation to your personal life? Have you or your parents dealt with troubles that resulted in adding to your spiritual strength—an ability to hang on? Unfortunately, this is not always the outcome. What did you learn from this experience (good or bad) to help you and your kids in the future?
2. Rahab was an Amorite who worshipped idols. Her faith was based on fear, yet she became a believer in God because of hearing of the wondrous things He had done for His people. Peter was a Jew, brought up under the Law of Moses and the influence of the Jewish traditions. He accepted Jesus as the Messiah and believed He was the Savior, though Peter did not fully understand the nature of the kingdom at first. What attributes did Rahab and Peter have that were displayed in the situations presented in chapter 1? Did their backgrounds play a part in their decisions? In spite of her history, Rahab appears to be a strong person. What grade would you give Peter? Why?

3. You and I are never past being tested either. There will always be the proverbial "fork in the road." Discuss the points in this chapter that prepare us and our kids for meeting these challenges and making the right decisions. How important is our faith and commitment to God in passing the "big test"? What are your thoughts on the need for self-evaluation to be able to confront the pitfalls we may have not yet encountered?
4. Where can we get some grit? Answer and give examples of the following ways and then discuss which way would be the most effective and why:
   a. Taught by lecture/books.
   b. Learned by observation of another person.
   c. Gained through fabricated scenarios.
5. There is an approximately fifty-year difference between the times in which Carrie Johnson and Steve Watts lived. In view of both economic and social dissimilarities in these periods, how might this have affected their developing tenacity in the face of their hardships? What does their tenacity to do what is right say about their character?
6. Though growing up far removed from the scenarios of the lives of Carrie and Steve, Haley, Rosalind, and Claire present a view of difficulties and temptations as we see them in the twenty-first century. Each mentions a form of social interaction for children:
   a. Haley: Letting others make decisions for them; passive living.
   b. Rosalind: Protecting them from uncomfortable situations.
   c. Claire: Having a proper relationship with those they are trying to teach.

In these contexts, what do you see as the overwhelming need in preparing this and future generations to have the perseverance to stand strong spiritually?

For Personal Use

Write down the most important concept you gained from chapter 1 in regard to developing spiritual fortitude in kids. You will be asked to do this for each chapter. Then personally review your answers at the conclusion of this twelve-lesson study. What did you learn about yourself? What can you pass on to the next generation(s)?

2

THE MOST IMPORTANT BODY PART: PARENTS PREPARE

Colleen

Conscientious parents, grandparents, and teachers have good ideas for influencing a child in their charge. They may even be on the cutting edge with their approaches. That's the easier part. The difficult part is following through on those outstanding ideas and goals. When you are rearing children, teaching children, or preparing to, you must analyze your ability to follow through and your level of self-discipline.

Now, everyone is self-disciplined when it comes to the tasks they've been accomplishing since childhood, when their parents taught them. Everyone is self-disciplined when highly motivated or when the reward comes in the short-term. You may get yourself to work every day or never miss filing your tax returns. That's admirable but not what I'm talking about. How do you fare on new dietary restrictions? New academic rigor? Can you do what should be done, when it's the right time, whether your heart is in it or not—whether there's a short-term benefit or not? Can you continue to practice a healthy habit whose rewards you won't feel for another forty years?

Where should you begin as a leader? It's not with the kids; start with yourself. You don't need to buy a book, but if you're a person who has to have a book, then buy one—but not one about kids. Buy a book about willpower, time management, or self-discipline. It's crucial that you be able to stick to your excellent resolutions for the long term if you want to direct the next generation to stay on track.

Your first action in that direction (and we'll remind you at the end of the chapter) is to develop a new habit that takes self-discipline and requires that you follow through indefinitely. It could be reading your Bible on a regular basis, maybe every other day for so many pages or minutes; it could be some other willpower endeavor. Then don't let yourself off the hook, no matter what. You will be developing for yourself one indispensable body part.

Humor and Body Parts

In the Bible, to illustrate the unity of the body of Christ, the apostle Paul brings forth in 1 Corinthians 12:12–21 an imaginary human body whose parts are at odds with each other. He resolves the humorous hypothetical conflict by stating, "The eye cannot say to the hand, 'I have no need of you'; nor again the head to the feet, 'I have no need of you'" (v. 21). The goal is for the body to function perfectly and achieve its greatest work. Paul never mentions backbone, but without it, these valuable body parts will accomplish nothing.

Nowhere is backbone more important than in the training of children. It is the engine providing offense to move them ahead and defense to clobber forces that encroach. You can possess a great deal of knowledge; you can have the most intelligent strategies and the best intentions, but if you can't follow through, your grand goals will evaporate.

Eye versus Backbone

Julie and Tim Estes provided their son, William, with an eye exam when he started kindergarten, and he passed with flying colors (Estes 2019). According to Julie, several years later, the same test revealed that he was legally blind in one eye. The eye was properly formed, but his brain did not respond to it. The diagnosis was amblyopia, or "lazy eye."

Several doctors examined William, with each contributing more information about his condition and prognosis. Occlusion therapy might improve his sight. If his problem had been caught at age two, it could have easily been cured. There is a window of time for children to be helped by this type of therapy; it closes around age nine. William was eight years old. He would have to wear a patch over his good eye to force the blind eye to develop and be acknowledged by his brain.

For the first three doctors, the mood was urgent but not demanding, with advice to try the easier routes first and see what happened. It was up to the parents whether to start the eye patch therapy then or wait until the summer in several months. That mood changed starkly when the Esteses saw their fourth doctor, an ophthalmologist out of Nashville. Her demeanor was dramatic, driving a sense of crisis and stressing imperative respect for the minute details of William's therapy. She in no way coddled him. When he told her he wanted to drive a Ford Mustang when he grew up, she said with a dooming delivery, "You'll never drive a Mustang if you don't wear your eye patch!"

This doctor bluntly told Julie that time was running out, and if she didn't adhere strictly to all aspects of his treatment, her son would always be impaired in one eye. If he should lose sight in his good eye, that would render him legally blind for life. It was enough to make everyone in the room crumble.

That's the introduction; we're just getting to the backbone part. Julie and Tim embarked on an arduous offensive to save their son's vision, despite William's resistance. Actually, resistance isn't the word—it was an all-out counteroffensive. The despised eye patch had to be applied perfectly, without even a pinhole of light penetrating. William was monitored constantly to ensure he didn't tamper with the patch in an effort to use his good eye. He wore the patch all day, every day at times. He opposed this with every trick, every argument he could throw at his parents. And I haven't gotten to the dilating eye drops.

William's good eye had to be completely disabled, or else his brain would never let the blind eye function. Julie and Tim had to hold William down to drip the dilation fluid into his eye several times a week. There was also an allergy drop administered, as needed, on a daily basis. He wailed as he melted onto the floor in despair. William had gotten along well enough before anyone knew one of his eyes didn't work. This wasn't life threatening. He wasn't in pain, but he was now suffering for an outcome far in the future and difficult to imagine. On top of all this was the stigma of wearing an eye patch to school and the toll it took on his academics.

Forcing William to use only his legally blind eye meant he was hampered in reading a page or the whiteboard. Many aspects of comprehension in the classroom were compromised at a critical time in his elementary grade Bible class and school education.

This may sound like a case where Julie and Tim had no choice but to insist on the therapy and enforce all details of it perfectly because the stakes were so high. However, other parents in the Esteses' situation backed down when their children resisted to the relentless therapy. That is why the eye specialist was dire in her outlook. She had seen the masses; she knew the routine. Even when a child's vision is hanging in the balance, many parents cave.

Tim and Julie did not cave. Remarkable was their dedication to William's Bible class learning. They wanted him to know God. Since he had trouble reading the digital slides projected on the classroom screen, Julie let him view the slides on her tablet computer close up. She also rewrote his Bible quiz questions so that they made better sense to him. She and Tim diligently drilled William on his scripture memory verses and checked his homework sheets to ensure they were completed correctly—even on vacation. It was a lot of fancy footwork but doubly important because of William's learning disability.

He is autistic. The blindness, the eye patch, the eye drops, and the doctors all occurred on top of autism. The Esteses also were working just as hard to make sure that William's twin brother, Phillip, was engaged in Bible class and comprehending God's word and also achieving in public school. Phillip is autistic as well. How much backbone does one couple have to have? Julie and Tim were already durable

Christians and self-disciplined individuals before they encountered their many challenges. Their kids are mighty fortunate.

Wrestling Match Now; Diploma Later

Balancing the duties and joys of life is a perpetual calculation, a give and take. People who have a long perspective of time, who can project very far into the future, are more adept at sacrificing today to enjoy more important rewards in the distant years. When Tim and Julie dreaded to but still pinned William down to administer his eye drops amid the sobbing—his, and perhaps theirs—they were fueled by their ability to see his future and their goals for him. Intensely dedicated to his spiritual and secular education, they were willing to have another dismal, stressful day if it meant he had a chance at gaining eyesight and all the capabilities associated with it.

Are you willing to do the repulsive, boring, or mentally challenging duties associated with childrearing to secure the highest rewards for your kids? What if the children resist—passionately and continually? Will you back off a little? Will you back down completely? When we first have children, it's fun to envision the ideal version of them in twenty years. Then reality rears up. Your kids don't have the desire or inclination to do the things you have in mind for them. They ignore your instructions and do it their way. They outright defy you. And you're not even past potty training yet.

Consider lofty goals like taking the gospel to lost souls or solving problems between Christians, like designing instruction for Bible class or cleaning up after sick people. Ideally, we would start conditioning our children for these endeavors from birth by teaching them Bible songs and stories and by enforcing strategies for getting along with siblings and playmates. It's difficult. They squirm away; they have no sense of the ultimate value of the song or story. The last thing they want to do is cooperate with their big brother. It's unpleasant work, and what's worse, there is little reward for many years.

That is one of the most profound lessons I learn from Julie and Tim Estes as they work tirelessly with their boys. The labor and emotional upheaval is big, with the rewards being very small and painfully slow now. Every so often there is great news or someone notices a big improvement in William's or Phillip's development, but on a daily basis, the benefits are difficult to see. This separates the grit from the quit.

Establish Your Position

The younger the kids are when you establish your position as the adult and leader, the better. However, wherever you are in this gig, now is the time to work on yourself—even if you are a grandparent or older teacher. Decide what kind of person you need to be, and then discipline and educate yourself to be that. Start by being solid on the principles and good habits you already possess. You must take time to contemplate your positions. Analyze why these things are important, and if you can't come up with a reason, be ready to back down, because if it takes work or unpleasantness or tediousness, kids will resist. You will back down. How will you react if your spouse resists or is without zeal or is wavering on these points?

Have your reasoning ready. It's not difficult, but it takes time and thought, something we have been trained to recoil from in the Digital Age. Computers have sped up so many processes and eliminated so much pondering and thinking that we feel put out if we have to analyze with our brains. We are chided for "thinking too much." Don't let anyone deter you with that tactic.

Take advantage of commute time or other extra time. Or secrete yourself away from people, computers, media, phones, and so on to decide what values you want to instill in your kids or students. Add new values and adjust your strategy as your experience and intellect expand. Your principles need to be deliberate, not just what feels right at the time. Then establish the reason behind your teachings so that your kids can't argue you down and you don't abandon your laudable aspirations.

For example, I've taken a lot of good-natured bashing from my husband and kids for the plain meals I serve. The arguments and scientific data are on the tip of my tongue when it is time to debate my culinary strategy. I am a good sport but stand my ground, because I know that in the long run, my family benefits from consuming just plain steamed vegetables and lean meat sans the rich sauces and sweet additives. If I had no conviction, or if I was cooking this way just because my mother taught me to, I would have conceded, to my family's disadvantage.

Haley

Having a backbone when it comes to raising children means you must have the right kind of backbone. The spine of a contortionist—bending to every whim of a child—is no good. Neither is spinal fusion—a rigid, narrow approach—the way to guide children to the Lord. Parenting often comes down to the Goldilocks Principle: there is a balanced place between extremes that is just right. And when it comes to the strong leadership of children, the Goldilocks Principle holds true.

Kids are smart. When they believe they can get what they want, they are a formidable force to make that happen. Only a strong backbone can withstand their nearly irresistible attacks, and it's best if that backbone is reinforced by two congruent spines—Mom's and Dad's. We often see examples of parental contortion in the cases of families unglued by divorce. Parents part ways, and children shuffle between them, taking advantage of the favor each parent desires from the children.

The following true example may sound familiar to you, because, sadly, it is very common. Sarah and Will (not their real names) were neighborhood playmates. Sarah invited Will to spend the day with her and her brother. During the playdate her dad, a divorced father, took them all to a toy store. His instructions when they entered were, "You can look around, but I'm not buying anything for you today." Sarah and her brother heard, but it didn't matter, because they had their father's number. He was divorced. He wanted his progeny to want to spend time with him and even prefer him to their mother. They knew that meant they could get whatever they wanted. Sarah and her brother told this to their friend, Will, and offered to prove it to him. "We don't really want it, but we can get our dad to buy us the most expensive thing in this store." That item was an electric kids' car.

Sarah's dad quickly lost his conviction to buy nothing. After weakly rejecting their request, he agreed to purchase the car. Will was amazed. These kids could truly bend an adult's backbone to their wishes. Before the purchase was made, Sarah and her brother told their dad they didn't really want it and that he didn't have to buy it.

But parents can go too far in the other direction if they teach their children to be dogmatic, having backbones that are fused and unable to adjust when necessary. This can be as harmful as a flimsy backbone to the future of a child's soul, because kids will pick up the parents' undesirable traits. Teaching children rigidity ill equips them for facing a devil who takes advantage of every weakness.

Continue to develop that sweet spot, that balanced stance between a yield sign and a stop sign. Practice firmness, but remember the Goldilocks Principle: provide necessary boundaries while affording opportunities to learn and exercise free will. You can get it "just right."

Rosalind

My mom reminds me that, as a child, when I was told to go do something I didn't want to do, I would slowly "slither" down the couch I was sitting on and end up in a pile on the floor. No matter how determined parents are, their kids will try to get out of just about every boring or difficult task. I know because I used to do it all the time! But slither or not, if my parents told me to do something, I knew that one way or the other, I was going to end up doing it.

Tantrums and arguments from children make it hard to stay strong—and easy to abandon the longstanding objective, whether it be physical health, spiritual strength, common sense in life, or academic accomplishment. Before you know it, the kid has turned the tables on you and is setting the standards for behavior.

I had a friend who, when presented with food at dinner that he did not want to eat, had only to take one bite and say, "No, thank you," and he was not required to eat any more. That was the policy in his home. Most kids would love to take one bite of lima beans, say, "No, thank you," and make a swift beeline for the dessert. Instead, in these moments, children can be taught the value of obedience, finishing a task, pushing through uncomfortable situations, and taking care of the physical body.

Parents, grandparents, teachers, neighbors, friends—it starts with you. We sometimes forget, but children are watching our every move, and they want to be like us. I was reminded of this recently when my two-year-old friend was sitting next to me in a worship service. I looked down to check on her and noticed that she was trying to cross her arms, which I had never seen her do before, so it caught my attention. Then I noticed that I had crossed my own arms, and it made sense.

Children imitate not only your physical actions but also the emotional, mental, and spiritual ones. When you set goals in your own life, be determined to follow through, and your children will notice. Maybe you feel that you have squandered opportunities in the past or didn't have the perseverance with your children you wish you had. I'm reminded of a favorite Chinese proverb: "The best time to plant a tree was twenty years ago. The second best time is now." Start today.

Claire

As a child, whether your parent has backbone or not isn't something that really crosses your mind. But you see the outgrowths—other kids getting to do things you wish you could do or others getting out of doing things you wish you didn't have to do. Sometimes your parents explain why they do things differently, and you understand but still want to fight it. For most children only hindsight shows the rewards of their parents' resolve.

For instance, it wasn't until I was in college and had roommates that I appreciated knowing how to keep house. These roommates had no experience or sense of responsibility in regard to taking out the trash, cleaning up something they had spilled, or cleaning the shower. I realized my parents had carefully prepared me to be a responsible and independent person.

My first internship boss told me I was very hardworking. It really struck him that I kept coming back for more assignments when I had finished my projects instead of waiting for him to realize I was ready for more. To me, my work ethic was second nature. I didn't always appreciate it at the time, but I was raised constantly putting my hands to the task and not finishing until the job was done properly.

I remember having the chore of cleaning the bathrooms. After tackling the grimy job, I would have to have my mom come and check to make sure I had cleaned thoroughly. If not, I would have to redo the streaky mirror or sanitize the forgotten underside of the toilet seat. After a while of this, I learned to do things right the first time and pay attention to detail.

It would have been much easier for Mom not to check my work or maybe even finish it herself after realizing how poor my effort was the first time. As a child, I didn't notice any difference from other kids when I had situations like this with my mom. I wasn't even aware of her persistence, but now I know my boss would have noticed the lack of it in me if my parents hadn't enforced their training.

My dad didn't allow anything to be done halfway. He often reminded us of Colossians 3:23: "And whatever you do, do it heartily, as to the Lord and not to men." I like how this verse is so applicable to every position in life. It reminds me to do my best in studying for a test. It reminds me to do my best even when my boss doesn't appreciate my work. I have a higher purpose than the earthly circumstances. Getting satisfaction from laboring for your boss will take you only so far. Knowing your work is of value to God will give you the empowerment to truly do your best. This verse reminds us not only of the inward motivation but also that our productivity shines God's light to others.

I have a friend whose parents never really talked about Santa Claus at Christmastime. The message his parents sent was, "We worked hard for the money to buy these presents for you." The point was that some old man named Santa doesn't just let you have this for free; we all have to toil and be thankful. This friend started a business at age fifteen, began saving, and then paid for his college and graduate school completely on his own, without debts or help from parents. He learned that things would never simply be given to him, and he took action. Without the mindset of his parents, he might not have learned the importance of appreciation and doing strenuous things.

Assignments

1. Develop a new habit that takes self-discipline and requires that you follow through indefinitely. Give this a lot of thought. It should be something that is important enough to improve your life but not so complicated or unpleasant that you know you'll give up. However, if it's too easy to do, it's probably too easy to not do. Choose something that you will actually do.
2. Answer and discuss with a partner the discussion questions below.
3. Continue to memorize Luke 4:1–14. Complete the memorization over the next month. Be able to recite it for a partner (who follows the scripture to check your words).

Chapter 2 Discussion Questions

1. Reread the sections "Eye versus Backbone" and "Wrestling Match Now; Diploma Later." Discuss how steadfast you would be under these kinds of circumstances. Could you hold on under this pressure? Do your kids call the shots in a confrontation? Julie and Tim have a tremendous amount of backbone. Do an honest self-examination of yours.
2. Evaluate and discuss the goals you have set out for your children: to be godly individuals, strong, independent, above average. Compare your aims with the examples cited by Haley, Rosalind, and Claire. How do you handle opposition to your authority? Do you allow your kids to argue with you that "everyone else can…" or "_______doesn't have to…"?

For Personal Use

Write down the most important concept you gained from chapter 2 in regard to developing spiritual resolve in kids. You will be asked to do this for each chapter. Then personally review your answers at the conclusion of this twelve-lesson study. What did you learn about yourself? What can you pass on to the next generation(s)?

3

TEACH, BUILD, MANEUVER, DEFEND

Colleen

Parents and teachers are both scouts and intel for their children. It's against nature for children to direct the adults. I have seen and heard about cases where adults allow the kids to advise them on how the relationship should work, how the household should operate, or what food to serve. It's not the children at the root of this reversal of authority—it's parents who are unwilling to assume the uncomfortable role of directing children and then sticking to it.

When I was a kid, I would not have joined the school band or endured braces on my teeth if I thought I could have talked my parents out of it. I am perpetually grateful they didn't back down. They were the adults; they could see the future benefits. I could see only the short-term inconvenience. God brings children into the world tiny and with no knowledge. Parents are large and full of knowledge and experience. Their job is to teach, build, maneuver, and defend, bringing the children into adulthood at full potential.

The Old Testament book of Nehemiah is the narrative of reestablishing Jerusalem under the leadership of Nehemiah and Ezra, and it's not a bad parallel to the way adults can teach, build, maneuver, and defend as leaders of the younger generation today.

To Teach

In Nehemiah, jumping to chapter 8, the demand is to reconstruct Israel morally and in regard to God as part of its return from captivity. Teaching is the foundational force in this transformation, in the same way it should be for anyone leading children. To appreciate this teaching, look first at its effect. Nehemiah 8:9 states that "all the people wept, when they heard the words of the Law." The teaching reaches into the hearts of the hearers and provokes them to mourn for how they have failed the Lord and for what they are missing. Further, the instruction results in a reminder of mercy from the leaders: "'Do not sorrow, for the joy of the Lord is your strength.' So the Levites quieted all the people, saying, 'Be still, for the day is holy; do not be grieved'" (Nehemiah 8:10–11). First comes remorse, then joy at knowing there is hope for redemption.

The next effect is a jolt to action, when the teaching reveals that Israel is deeply delinquent in observing the ceremonies of the Law of Moses. Therefore, they keep the Feast of Tabernacles, dwelling outside in temporary structures, and even rejoice about it because they know it pleases God.

The people are so jolted that they agree to upset the local economy by reinstating restrictions on Sabbath commerce, and they begin to financially support the priesthood and the temple. The teaching brings emotions of mourning, weeping, rejoicing, and gladness that turn to action. This is precisely what parents and all who teach the gospel are trying to evoke when they open the Bible to others.

Now back up to the beginning of Nehemiah 8, when "the people gathered together as one man in the open square" (v. 1). Here is how the teaching starts—with people. People who know the Law, like Ezra, who "had prepared his heart to seek the Law of the Lord, and to do it, and to teach statutes and ordinances in Israel" (Ezra 7:10). Ezra opens the book and reads as the people are listening and attentive and purposeful.

It doesn't stop there. The people need something more, some clarification. The Levites "helped the people to understand the Law;

and the people stood in their place. So they read distinctly from the book, in the Law of God; and they gave the sense, and helped them to understand the reading" (Nehemiah 8:7–8). As the teachers gave "the sense" in Nehemiah's day, so we must do the same in our day for whomever we teach. As Ezra prepared, so must we prepare.

To Build

We are not just teaching our children information—we are building them, developing them to operate on that information and wisdom at the right time and under pressure. Now rewind to Nehemiah chapter 2, where Nehemiah, the other leaders, and the people determine to build the destroyed wall of Jerusalem. This episode figuratively parallels the building of our children and the tenacity adults are required to muster in order to push through opposition to lead with fortitude and singlemindedness.

The construction project begins on a note of optimism and heartening reliance on God as the people "set their hands to this good work" (Nehemiah 2:18). Right out of the gate, there is opposition from the neighbors. Non-Jews Sanballat, Tobiah, and Geshem make fun and deride the builders, accusing them of rebellion. Nehemiah answers fearlessly that the "God of heaven Himself will prosper us" (2:20). Imagine people and organizations that would chip away at your resolve in leading children toward godliness.

The wall construction rolls along as the men and women make real progress with their tools, as the naysayers hammer home their message of contempt. Even with constant disturbances, the workers tirelessly advance in their architecture project. Their minds are focused on gradually closing the gaps. The strategy is simple: Don't stop.

We also must close the gaps as we develop our children and stay on duty. For parents it calls for a keen awareness that few adults are inclined to invest in their young ones. Many hand off the job to someone else. There's a temptation for parents to let time spent on building their children get out of balance with time they spend in their own pursuits. How do I know? I have been adept at it myself.

Adults have many legitimate responsibilities, and they also have personal interests. The key is balancing these with the towering obligation to spend adequate time and attention on nurturing our children. I don't have an airtight formula for ensuring perfect balance, but I can offer two suggestions for assessing your particular situation and attending better. Calculate hours spent, and assess actual interaction.

First, try to make an objective appraisal of how many hours you spend paying attention to your kids in an average week. Not staring at a screen together. Not reading the news while they practice their piano. This is you talking or playing or reading, and so on with your child, where there is some kind of communication.

School and work time can chew up the best hours of the day, so when you calculate, you may get a grim sum. If you do, use that as the point where you promise to do better—for life. Whatever you do, don't use fuzzy reasoning to make a dismal number better than it is by calling a few minutes a day "quality time." Please, if it's bad news, let it sink in. Determine to spend more time with your kids, and tell others so that it will be more difficult for you to quit. You will never regret the time you spend with your kids.

Let me say that again. You will never regret the time you spend with your kids. You may regret spending time doing other things, but not that. And it pays treasures' worth of return on investment.

Second, take some quiet time to think about the quality of the communication and activities you share with your kids in an average week. Are you present but your spouse and kids are doing the interacting? Are you on your phone while the children play? If you're a grandparent, do you talk with the adults while the grandchildren go off to play on their own? Is the TV a loud buttinsky to your relationship with your kids?

Making a change in the way you attend to your children may not come easily, but it disburses big dividends. And when you feel those dividends, hang onto them tightly. Don't slide back into old patterns.

I knew a father with a whole bunch of kids. On a regular basis, when he came home from work, he went straight to the backyard and played sports with his kids, laughing and chasing with even the tiny ones. Then he had a bunch more kids. I rarely saw him outside with them anymore. Extraordinary start—maybe it was difficult to follow through.

To Maneuver

Back to Nehemiah, we see how, after hearing that the outsiders had planned a physical attack to stop the building, the workers maneuver in response yet plow ahead with their number-one goal—finishing the wall:

> So we labored in the work, and half of the men held the spears from daybreak until the stars appeared. At the same time I also said to the people, "Let each man and his servant stay at night in Jerusalem, that they may be our guard by night and a working party by day." So neither I, my brethren, my servants, nor the men of the guard who followed me took off our clothes, except that everyone took them off for washing. (Nehemiah 4:21–23)

This reminds me of parents with a newborn baby—on duty always and wearing yesterday's clothes. As with new parents, even though there are challenges—and big ones—the laborers entertain no notion of abandoning and running for their lives. Instead they remain in place, prepared.

Also, Nehemiah and his personal group apparently are sleeping in their clothes so that they'll be ready to get up even if a raid comes in the middle of the night. To maneuver proactively is also what Carrie Johnson, our earlier example, endeavored to do. She had not been faithful to God early in her adult life. To prevent that from happening to her family, she made sure her two daughters grew up with a proper respect for God, His word, and worship to Him.

For example, in preparation for Bible class and worship on Sunday, every Saturday night Carrie ensured the girls' Bible lesson questions were answered correctly. The girls took baths, rolled their hair, polished their shoes, and washed the shoestrings. Carrie saved scarce money to buy Bible dictionaries, concordances, and Bible commentaries and to subscribe to church periodicals to educate her children to have their own faith, not just hers.

To Defend

When it becomes apparent to Nehemiah that the non-Jews could strike at any time, workers on the actual wall continue with one hand and grip a weapon with the other, a sword at each person's side. Nehemiah exhorts, "Do not be afraid of them. Remember the Lord, great and awesome, and fight for your brethren, your sons, your daughters, your wives, and your houses" (4:14). If our children are the walls, we are the builders, the strategists, and the defenders. Anything that hijacks our efforts is Sanballat & Company. That would be those who want your children's time and their minds through entertainment, video games, and the next social media update. The opposition could be desires to seek comfort or sex or to blend in with society. When these attacks and diversions appear, leave no place unguarded, using extreme vigilance and all resources.

Idle kids can be soft targets for Satan. When distractions are at every turn, it's necessary to be proactive to train children to be busy doing the Lord's work. I know some women who stepped up to lead teenage girls in a group called the Salt Shakers, a reference to Jesus's admonition that "You are the salt of the earth" (Matthew 5:13). The adult leaders guide the girls to perform good deeds. They teach the girls to be self-starters. They bring in Christian speakers to influence the girls. In so doing, the leaders rally strength in numbers and defend against threats.

We Build, We Fight

During World War II, civilian contractors built advance bases for the military all over the world ("Seabee History" 2015). There was a problem in case of attack, though, since these workers were not soldiers.

If they fought in any way, they were classified as guerillas under international law, and they could be immediately executed. That's why the United States established a new branch under the Navy that could build and fight as military personnel. We know them as the Seabees.

The Seabees' motto is "We build, we fight," and doesn't this sound relevant to our discussion? We are the advance base for our children. We go in first and prepare for the work and the defense. We build and we fight too.

In 1944 the Seabees posted a sign on Bougainville Island in the South Pacific Ocean. It read, "The difficult we do now. The impossible takes a little longer" (Reed 2019).

Haley

Yes, we build, we fight. Parents build durable, idealistic, and godly armaments to defend their children from the devil. They fight the apparent forces in pursuit of children's souls. However, in this fight not all destructive forces are those obvious ones that come from outside in the uniform of Satan's army. The threats from within can be subtle, with the power to derail your noble goals.

As I look back on my upbringing, I remember having seen some of this friendly fire. At the time I didn't recognize it as such, but having grown older and reflected on the past, I have begun to see that there are people on your side who may not support the good intentions you have for training your children. Lacking that support adds to the burdens of childrearing and makes your backbone all the more necessary.

My parents put considerable effort into molding my sisters and me into capable, thoughtful, and wise people. Like almost all of you reading this, now that I'm grown, I appreciate that effort and even the discipline I received, because I see how it came together to build admirable qualities in me. But when my parents were building, they required foresight—a vision of what their work would do. The problem was, not all of our family and friends had the same foresight. People on my parents' team might have had the same goals—that my sisters and I would be capable, thoughtful, and wise—but they didn't see that those goals are reached only through great effort. They agreed on the goals but resisted the trouble.

My sisters and I each participated in People to People. It's a program that takes kids from the US to visit new parts of the world to broaden their horizons. An exemplary program, right? Well, not everyone in the extended family thought so. One older relative voiced disapproval of our parents' decision to let us travel without family, imagining the risks—like mad cow disease—as probable outcomes. One grandmother's rational mind said, "Yes, that is a commendable program," but in her weaker moments, she was scared to death. My parents no doubt recognized the risks, but they kept their sights on the more likely, productive outcomes of sending their daughters to foreign lands. Despite our relatives' fears, we forged ahead, and each of us became world travelers.

That trip was one of the most meaningful things my parents did to raise me to be informed and independent. I see that now. My relatives probably recognized that, too, when they saw the adult I became. But hindsight won't give you the opportunity to raise your children again. You must resolve to trust your foresight and strengthen that resolve when the people who are close to you chip, chip, chip away at it.

Disloyalty inside the Walls

Think back to our example of Nehemiah when he leads the Israelites in rebuilding Jerusalem and defending it "with their swords, their spears, and their bows" (Nehemiah 4:13). The people, with their weapons and God's support, keep Israel's numerous enemies out of the city. But the danger isn't only from the outside. Some Israelites within the walls are working for the cause and also harboring the enemy.

There is a man named Eliashib in Nehemiah 13. He is one of those Israelites. He lets the enemy infiltrate the walls by making a room for Tobiah—one of the more outspoken outsiders trying to halt construction—to stay in the city. And where is that room? It is in the temple. The temple. The most prominent place in Jerusalem. The house of God. It doesn't stop there. Eliashib is no humble, common man looking for an opportunity to profit. He is a priest. He has a stake in the outcome of the rebuilding and only stands to benefit if Jerusalem grows and thrives, yet he undermines the progress by welcoming the enemy.

When he discovers Eliashib's corruption, Nehemiah doesn't withdraw from his intentions. He does not lose course when he faces the fact that a spiritual leader of the people is impeding progress. He uses that moral fiber of his and steadfastly redoubles his efforts, remembering his vision for the restoration of Jerusalem.

Also, at the beginning of Nehemiah, the writer gets permission from King Artaxerxes to rebuild the city of his fathers that he loves. It is a noble cause but a difficult one, and the difficulty must be very discouraging. Even the people who are supposed to help him lead in rebuilding the city—the priests—are lukewarm and weak, and they often demoralize him. However, Nehemiah's work is ultimately successful. Eventually his persistence pays off. The wall stands, and Israel inhabits the city again.

Lukewarm Attitudes within the Ranks

My parents resisted lukewarm attitudes and sometimes outright resistance as they led their children in working today to gain a big reward in the distant future. Here's an example. When I was in school, my mom made me practice my trumpet over the summer, unlike most other students. Now, anybody who's been in school symphonic band knows that most kids close their horn cases in May, and the instruments get no oxygen until the school year starts again. What drool was in the horn turns into a dry, musty film, and the reeds wax brittle. They get no light whatsoever. Band directors shiver to think of the flabby lips walking through the door in the fall. Or so we thought.

One day my mom saw my band director during summer break, and as they were talking, she mentioned she'd made me practice. And was he pleased that there would be one trumpet player who could still squeak out an A above the staff? His response was, "I'm sorry."

Even some of those who are supposed to share your goals are just hirelings. They aren't invested in your child's future like you are. Their vision for your child doesn't include solos and music scholarships. Have the determination to be the advocate for your children and provide the pressure that gives them growth when nobody else wants to endure the headache of raising them—and making them practice.

Take inspiration from Nehemiah, a man with a firm stance. Friendly fire didn't deter him in his high standard. So don't let resistance within the ranks discourage you as you raise your children in wise ways. You may have to wait ten, fifteen, twenty years before those close to you who subtly opposed you see that the work you put in for your children paid off. And those ten, fifteen, or twenty years will be your most challenging. If you don't feel the support from your team, it's easy to compromise on your plans to raise above average children. That's why your backbone is indeed your most important body part. Without it, in-laws, parents, friends, and even brothers and sisters in Christ can apply pressures that obscure your foresight. They can cause you to back down. Use your willpower to fight for the work you do for your children. It will pay off. If not in this lifetime, in the next.

Rosalind

After I woke up from a recent major surgery, my surgeon advised that on the next day I needed to start getting up out of bed and start trying to walk. I was told that a physical therapist would visit and help me get out of bed. The next day came and went with no sign of a therapist. Knowing how important it is to start moving after surgery, my family members began regularly asking the hospital staff when a physical therapist would arrive. No one could say for sure, so we waited, kept inquiring about it, and Easter Sunday came to a close without me taking one step. Although I knew the importance of getting up, I really did not want to. Given the pain and fatigue after surgery, I was much happier to stay right where I was, in bed. But my team of cheerleaders knew better.

The following day, Monday, finally brought the arrival of a therapist. We found out that because the day before had been Easter, the therapy department was short-staffed. Just like with my sister's less-than-thrilled band director, who should have been her biggest supporter, the PT department was not as invested in me as my own family. However, the physical therapists proved to be extremely helpful. The very first skill the therapist taught me was how to get out of my bed, a seemingly simple undertaking. Considering the sizeable incision in my abdomen, getting up without straining was difficult. But it was the foundation for the rest of therapy, creating a basis for the next levels of strengthening.

Just as with recovering from surgery or an injury, training children to love the Lord begins with a strong foundation. They won't want to, but you have to get them out of bed, so to speak. I'm reminded of the wise and foolish builders in Matthew 7. The wise man constructed his house on a solid foundation, while the foolish man did so on an unsteady one, leading to a disastrous fall of the foolish man's home. Jesus taught that those who hear His words and practice them are wise and have a sturdy foundation in Him. Building that firm base in children comes from adults who love them, teach them, care deeply for the outcome of their souls, and refuse to let spiritual homes be built on the beach.

On the first time out of bed after my operation, I made it only to a nearby chair. But soon enough I could slowly walk up and down the hallway, up a flight of stairs, and to the car to go home. When building a strong spiritual foundation for children, start with small steps, rejoice in the victories, and continue pressing forward. Just as the people building the Jerusalem wall in Nehemiah had to set in their minds not to stop, you must work to keep the children in your life moving toward their eternal goal of a home in heaven, step by step.

Claire

I recently overheard a classmate speaking disrespectfully to someone over the phone. By the tone and disparaging remarks, I thought it must be some kind of banter with a brother. But as the conversation went on, I realized it wasn't really banter. It was coarse speech, and the person on the other end of the line was his dad. It struck me because this was a person I considered a friend. He had always been kind to me. How could he be so ugly to someone as honored as his father?

The point is, children can be disciplined in one area and not in another. They know what they can get away with, but parents are there to come in from all angles with them. How might parents prevent disrespectful words and actions coming from their children? I advocate nipping the first inklings of disrespectful speech and behavior in the bud from the earliest age. If children are allowed to be even slightly discourteous in any way toward their parents, it is up to the adults to make quick correction.

It isn't only parents who make their mark on the next generation spiritually. In 2 Timothy 1:5, Paul tells us that Timothy's grandmother was a spiritual influence on Timothy, and I can identify with this. My grandparents and other family members helped to teach, build, maneuver, and defend in a similar way. I would stay at my grandparents' house in another town from time to time. Many summers they would invite me over to attend vacation Bible school (VBS). When I was older, I began helping to teach and prepare meaningful lessons with my aunts for VBS at their church. This also gave me ideas for teaching at my home church.

Often, grandparents don't want to be the "bad guy," and they let children act up or behave selfishly while under their care. They want to spoil them. My grandparents made sure we behaved and didn't throw away our manners simply because our parents weren't around (and Granny and Papa were fun too). Their Christian example was immense. Included in that was the many times I accompanied my grandmother to visit the elderly. It helped me to understand the brevity of life, how to talk to adults, and to realize the importance of caring for people no matter whether they are relevant to my age or not.

My grandfather gave me the example of one who shared with any and all, whether they were asking for it or not. He was an accomplished cook and woodworker. For him being a good steward meant using his cooking skills to bring Christians and non-Christians together regularly over a meal, many being people he had met only once and invited on the spot. It also meant making things out of wood to give to others and fixing people's old, broken-down furniture.

Both of my grandparents showed us that part of defending was being good stewards of our money. They were fairly simple people, living well below their means but giving freely of their blessings to others. Though my grandparents have passed away, it is left to me, like Timothy, to "continue in the things which you have learned and been assured of, knowing from whom you have learned them" (2 Timothy 3:14).

Assignments

1. How are things going with the assignment from chapter 2 to take on a new habit? Continue to develop that new habit that takes self-discipline and requires that you follow through indefinitely. If you have trouble starting, come up with something very simple, and when you master that, add a little more complexity.
2. Sit down with a pen and paper and make an objective appraisal of how many hours you spend paying attention to your kids in an average week. Then think deeply about the quality of the communication and activities you share with your kids in an average week. Analyze all this and write down what may be lacking and what you will do to improve.
3. Continue to memorize Luke 4:1–14. Be able to recite it for a partner (who follows the scripture to check your words). How about encouraging your kids or students to memorize it too?

Chapter 3 Discussion Questions

1. How well do you communicate with your children? Think about the hours spent at school and/or work, where there are teachers, peers, playmates, coworkers, etc. who can undermine the foundations you are working to instill in your kids. Give serious thought to Assignment #2. Use the examples of the Israelites in Nehemiah's day as a reminder of the effects of opposition from those who are not like-minded.
2. What steps are you taking to ensure that your children have a proper view of God? He is to have first place in our hearts and lives. Is your Sunday morning a scramble to find misplaced Bibles and lesson books? Are lesson assignments done in the car on the way to class? What does this scene indicate to your kids about God's position in their lives?

3. What principles are you establishing in making rules and following through with them? Do you first impress the importance of being pleasing to God in all things? Look at some scriptures that bear this out (e.g., 2 Corinthians 5:9; Ephesians 5:10; Ephesians 6:5–8; Colossians 1:10; Colossians 3:23). Why should this be fundamental to your training?

For Personal Use

Write down the most important concept you gained from chapter 3 in regard to developing spiritual courage in kids. You will be asked to do this for each chapter. Then personally review your answers at the conclusion of this twelve-lesson study. What did you learn about yourself? What can you pass on to the next generation(s)?

4

THE HEART OF A CHILD

Colleen

"You'll have to get the shotgun out," said the doctor. My husband groaned. They were lamenting the headaches of raising daughters and fending off the boys. And we hadn't even checked out of the hospital with our newborn baby girl. Some of us approach parenthood with a long view to the future. Others want to hold close those charming few years of childhood, not worrying too much about graduation and college and—dating.

No matter your particular camp, children are meant to change, to transform. It would be against nature to view them in any other way. Proverbs 22:15 confirms, "Foolishness is bound up in the heart of a child; The rod of correction will drive it far from him." A colleague has quoted this to me book, chapter, and verse. He has five young children. Now I'm not suggesting a Dickensian plot, here, but a sense of reality. I've been a child, reared three, and taught many in Bible class. I've seen it to be true that kids are drawn to anything fun, pleasant, or comforting and anything novel or that promises a short-term reward. Children are averse to work, pain, tediousness, or anything involving exertion without a tangible reward in sight. That rod might be various kinds of correction; most kids don't like it. I know I didn't and still don't.

In 1 Corinthians 13, childhood is brought into an argument as an analogy for things useful yet frail and about to evaporate when it is time. In this passage the apostle Paul touts the superiority of love as an attribute of Christians. Prophecies, tongues, and knowledge will run their course and cease. In heaven when the smoke clears, of the four, only love will remain to be counted on. Then Paul writes, "When I was a child, I spoke as a child, I understood as a child, I thought as a child; but when I became a man, I put away childish things. For now we see in a mirror, dimly, but then face to face. Now I know in part, but then I shall know just as I also am known" (v. 11–12). Get the most out of prophecies, tongues, knowledge—and, yes, childhood—but understand that they are feeble compared to what will last. In heaven, love stands beyond prophecy, tongues, and knowledge. On Earth, adulthood stands beyond childhood.

For our kids, aversion to work, pain, tediousness, discomfort, exertion without clear immediate benefit, and so on begins to sink their tiny ship little by little from day one. It would serve a person much better to learn as a toddler than as a twenty-five-year-old that these aversions must be vanquished and unveiled as the shams they are if we are going to accomplish anything in service to Christ. It's much easier to train a baby than to deprogram someone who has years of experience and conditioning in avoiding difficulty and seeking a cushy pillow. Few would invite uncomfortable conditions, but the most productive among us ignore them in order to achieve the objective. So start when the kids are babies.

Bring Up a Worthy One

For those who want to raise a worthy woman or man from that infant, there's an exceptional role model in action in Proverbs 31:10–31. I think she must be at work even when my Bible is closed. This excellent woman teaches us how to accomplish a lot—and how to ignore a lot. This no doubt contributes to the reason her husband trusts her. It's just easier for all of us to feel secure with a persevering mate. He knows that inconveniences will not stop his wife from managing her work and her integrity.

Distance doesn't get in the way of her procuring the groceries she chooses as "she brings her food from afar" (v. 14). Darkness? No problem. Getting up very early in the morning? Not a consideration as "she also rises while it is yet night" (v. 15). Do the elements slow her down? No, "she is not afraid of snow for her household, for all her household is clothed with scarlet" (v. 21). Any of these factors could be excuses for deferring or begging out of work. This woman doesn't make excuses, and she doesn't shrink from reaching decisions, even complicated ones where she could lose money. "She considers a field and buys it; From her profits she plants a vineyard" (v. 16). One factor that bolsters her confidence is planning, which requires work. The "bread of idleness" (v. 27) is not on her menu.

Bring these considerations to your child. To instill this kind of "can do" philosophy, parents can't be sissies. If you are looking for a reason to avoid doing what you should do, you will find one. Examine yourself and see what kind of example you are. If your parents didn't have a strong work ethic or if they were soft individuals, it may be more difficult for you to recognize a lack of self-discipline in yourself. In this case maybe you have a family member or friend who can exemplify what you want to be. It could be someone who came of age in another era, when there was patience for neither life's obstacles nor weaklings.

Along with showing your kids how to get their hands dirty, teach them to brave the elements. Of course, the worthy woman was able to charge into the snow with her family because they had adequate clothing. A long walk in the rain wearing the right coat and shoes is a delight. Same for playing in the snow. Make sure all of you have suitable clothing, and then go outside. If your children are not used to playing outdoors for long periods of time, they may have to be conditioned to do it.

Going outside in the dark is another way to sidestep the passive couch inside. Playing tag and hide-and-go-seek in the dark is exciting and a little on the daring side for children. Also, take time to look up at the night sky with them, especially to witness celestial wonders that come in the inconvenient, cold morning hours. My husband, Wally, has been the prodder for the girls and me to enjoy the outdoors and to look up at the stars. Remember to look down at the bugs, rocks, and green growing things too.

Sometimes not having the best clothing or gear demonstrates to kids that it's the activities themselves and their companions that give deep meaning to life. For instance, the only items you need to play basketball are decent shoes, a good ball, and a goal. No, I take that back. I'm pretty sure I remember playing with slick, holey shoes and a flat ball. Oh, and the goal was a loop of garden hose nailed up on the side of the summer kitchen. For baseball, the ball was a beat up, dried out wad that could hardly be discerned because it was so grass- and dirt-stained. The bases were pieces of cardboard if you were lucky—if not, then sticks. One friend said he played stickball with a duct-tape ball and a broomstick. His bases were pine trees. Be careful sliding in that case.

My sister, Sheila, recently sponsored a weeklong "Grandma Camp" with eight of her grandchildren, ages three to eleven. All but two of them spent the night for that week. No video games allowed. They identified bugs, rode bikes, went swimming, and played kickball and whiffle ball. They put on a talent show for their extended family. They bickered. They made bracelets. Three boys learned to knit. Some chickened out of the talent show; some pressed on. They asked to watch TV, but the whole week they watched only a few hours of TV, one feature being an adaptation of *The Adventures of Tom Sawyer* to prepare them to read the novel. They played hide-and-go-seek in the dark. They learned to call, "A bushel of wheat, a bushel of rye, if you're not ready, holler 'Aye.'" The men joined in the fun when they got home from work.

The lesson? Rain, dark, cold, early morning, makeshift sports gear, stage fright—you name it—are quite benign and in no way worthy of standing in the way of our activities. These could be any endeavors when kids are growing up. The important part is to transfer to their spiritual tasks the brave, unstoppable stance they are developing. Perceived barriers lose their potency when viewed by people who are used to driving action in all facets of their lives. I know a boy who has that point of view. He became a Christian at a young age. When it was his turn to read scripture in the worship service, he was way too short to be seen behind the lectern. Did he shrink from the task? No way. He confidently climbed up on a stool and read his scripture without flinching or showing any self-consciousness. That's a worthy guy.

Adversity by Design

The woman of Proverbs 31 is proactive. The satisfactory situations she executes for her family, the community, and herself are possible because she understands the consequences of bad judgment. You might say the whole passage about her is a lesson in cause and effect. She chooses the action with a view to the desirable result. Regrettably, we all take the wrong route sometimes, and the consequences sting. It's difficult to ignore a sting or to forget it, so we learn not to take that wrong route ever again.

However, not all parents have the stomach for watching their children suffer the consequences of their own actions. Or it may be that some parents get such a charge out of comforting and eliciting smiles from their children that they duck the obligation to let the chips fall where they may. Various factors weigh into the judgment of when to intervene or even shield children from consequences. Are those consequences extremely severe? Has the child been warned repeatedly? It is complicated, and each situation is different. I boiled down three considerations that can help conscientious parents pay more attention to the ramifications of their intervention or lack of it, whichever way they choose to go:

1. Mistakes and pain are valuable elements of learning. We all can quickly think of a painful episode that taught a lifelong lesson, like the time I left my new, nifty bike out in the yard

all night and someone stole it. I didn't get another bike for several years.

2. The younger we are when we learn that our parents are right, the better. When I was little, my mom said the unsweetened chocolate on the counter tasted bad, and I didn't believe her. When she left the room, I bit off a piece and chewed. That horribly bitter taste taught me first-hand information that reminded me of my mom's warning.
3. Sisters and brothers learn valuable lessons from siblings' mess-ups. If you're a younger brother or sister, you probably have lots of examples of this.

I got into a scrape one time in the seventh grade. Some boy was being yelled at by the teacher, which put her in a prickly mood. She told me if I didn't wipe the smile off my face, she would paddle me. Those words went all the way from my ears down to my toes, ricocheted up, and jump-started my heart. Then she said I had to come back and talk to her the next day. I wasn't used to getting screamed at or being in trouble. Ahead of me were twenty-four hours of torment to await my fate. I would have done just about anything to squirm off this hook. I would have preferred a meeting with the bride of Frankenstein.

That night I asked my mom to call the teacher on the phone and try to get me out of my mess, which she did—try. This shrewd and unmerciful teacher wasn't buying it. No budging. I met with her the next day. She scolded me; I didn't get paddled. However, I did get something I needed—a bracing reality check and a shot of humility. My mom couldn't bear to see me on trial by ordeal, but the teacher—whether out of love or amusement—was willing to watch me writhe. This fright did teach me what I needed to do—master my poker face and stay out of the way when other kids got into trouble. In seriousness, I learned to be a little less silly and to conduct myself with better self-awareness, now knowing that not everyone thinks I'm so cute.

Unfortunately, some training opportunities are scrapped, like this one that popped up a few years ago. After school one of my daughters was met by some students who told her they saw a driver hit her vehicle in the parking lot. They said the driver put her finger to her lips in a "shh" sign as she drove away from the scene. I told my husband I was going to call the girl's parents and get them to pay for the damage to our vehicle. He said they would never pay. Maybe not, but I wanted to try.

When I got the father of the driver on the phone, I asked him if his daughter had had a car accident. "No," he said definitively. I asked him if he could check just to make sure. He checked, found out the truth, and then apologized to me, pledging to pay for the damage. Flush with hope in the human race—and with a little smugness—I told my husband that the culprit's family would be fixing our vehicle. He wasn't swallowing it, and those cynics among you are probably wearing a wry smile just now. I'm humbled to say the father of the malevolent driver never called me back. Not a peep. No—fix—truck.

Now, ours was an elderly Ford Ranger, and there wasn't much damage, not enough to lose sleep over. However, that teenage hit-and-run driver I am concerned about. I don't know her personally. You don't either, which is convenient, because we have no reason to defend or criticize. We can be objective and make pretty astute projections on what the incident may have taught a young person who gets away with something like this. As a parent what would you have done? Truly contemplate this question.

I fear for a young driver caught in something far weightier in the future because of failure to suffer the consequences of a parking-lot jalopy dent. Imagine a father getting a call from his teenage driver, who is at the scene of a serious car accident. The child reveals that she was texting moments before impact. How will the two dodge this predicament when there's possible jail time in the mix?

Train Up a Child

Ken Kuykendall's parents couldn't have known the circumstances he would endure later in life, but they undergirded their son with faith, emotional strength, and self-discipline that sustained many blows unbroken. Ken advises, "Be prepared for death at all times. Live each day as if it were your last! Ask yourself this question: 'What would I do today if I knew it were my last?'" (Kuykendall 2018). Being reared in a Christian home was key in preparing Ken for what crouched ahead decades later. He says,

> My parents never tried to shield me from adversity. Their example was one of trusting in God to help us weather the storms of life. Daily Bible reading was a regular practice in our family. They were also strict, but I knew that they loved me. I knew the consequences of disobedience. Unlike many parents today, my father always said if we got a spanking at school, we would get another one when we got home.

As a boy, Ken saw the ugly side of aging. His elderly aunt moved in with his family, and over the next few years, her health deteriorated until she died. The Kuykendalls allowed their kids to witness her struggling moments and to understand them as just a part of life to endure.

Ken's parents also taught him to pray his own heartfelt prayers, especially at bedtime. His father set an exceptional example in this as he prayed for one complete hour each night before bedtime, prohibiting phone calls and other interruptions during prayers.

Ken grew to adulthood and married. In 1970, at age thirty, his wife, Frilly, was near death from an incurable genetic disorder—mitochondrial encephalopathy, lactic acidosis, and stroke-like episodes (MELAS). Doctors advised Ken that she had only a 10-percent chance to live through surgery, and if she did, she would have only a 10-percent chance to live for two weeks. Ken called several Christians to pray for her, trusting that she would get well. The prayers were answered with a big "Yes." Frilly was given thirty more years. The couple brought up two faithful children, Kevin and Kerri.

Then, in 1996, death remembered the Kuykendalls. Their first granddaughter, Kara Beth Swanson, died, having been born three months early and in critical condition. In the year 2000, Frilly became ill, and after a three-month hospital stay, doctors advised Ken to take her off the ventilator. Neither option was easy. She died within twenty minutes. If you want to discuss the particulars of living wills and do-not-resuscitate (DNR) orders, Ken is your man—a dubious honor but one his parents equipped him to bear from childhood.

Ken had the courage to speak at Frilly's funeral and became stronger for his experiences, because, as he says, "If you are a Christian, it should increase your faith; you really don't have a choice." There were more speaking engagements coming.

Ken's daughter, Kerri, at age thirty-seven, became ill from the same disorder that struck her mother. In 2007 Kerri was in the hospital intensive care unit. Ken and his second wife, Charlene, prayed for Kerri. Then his son, Kevin, had a seizure. Ken says, "We had been praying for Kerri to improve, but instead Kevin got sick. Charlene and I didn't know what to pray for but realized that we must trust God."

Kerri was taken off the ventilator in 2007 and died a few hours later amid the melody of hymns, scripture reading, and prayers. Her brother, Kevin, died the next year at age forty-two of the same syndrome that had taken Kerri and Frilly. Ken's opening remark at both his children's funerals was, "This was not supposed to happen! Parents are not supposed to bury their children!" He surely missed many joys of life that husbands and fathers typically plan for, but his analysis of the situation is that he got what really matters—the abiding peace that Frilly, baby Kara, Kerri, and Kevin are all in paradise.

This peace was sown as seed by his parents from infancy. "Train up a child in the way he should go, And when he is old he will not depart from it" (Proverbs 22:6). Ken needed the pain of hardship, humility, physical discomfort, etc. that his mother and father allowed him to brace against and experience. Their little stone was tumbled attentively, and his parents got what really mattered because, as Ken puts it, although he did lose his family, he kept his faith.

Haley

There's a well-known proverb—even outside the church—that says, "He who spares his rod hates his son" (Proverbs 13:24). That rod is an important part of the polishing process. The verse doesn't end there, though. It continues, "But he who loves him disciplines him promptly." Discipline includes the rod—punishment—but it also includes perpetuating the good. Discipline is a correction. Whether a child has done something wrong and needs to be set straight or could do a good thing better, discipline turns the child to face the more perfect way. Don't stop at correcting wrong; do more to perpetuate right.

The point of children is not to have them; it's to develop them into responsible Christians who follow God's law and spread the good news. They start as little people so that parents can teach them what they need to know in adulthood. It's fortunate that it works this way. Think about how difficult it would be to raise a child who has the stubborn mind of an adult.

In their pliable state, children are very willing to do what you want them to do. It's rare that a child in Bible class doesn't want to do right. They love God, they want to learn about Him, and their consciences are powerful to guide them in the right way. So it's easy for parents to look at their children and think, "Little Billy is such a good person. He goes to Bible class and loves to learn. He wants to be a preacher when he grows up. He doesn't do things that are wrong, so I don't need to use that rod from Proverbs 13:24."

Maybe Billy's parents don't need the rod right now, but they still need to discipline. They must do more to keep him on the wise path. While a child is young, he does what his parents want him to. When he grows up, however, he exerts his own will. To ensure that a grown child will exercise his desire in the right manner, a parent can't afford to ignore teaching more of the correct way now.

Here's a way you can do more to help prepare your children to be faithful attendees of the assembly: make church attendance a priority on vacation. Do this, and you will teach them the following lessons:

- Nothing gets in the way of your regular worship. Not distance. Not being away from the local church of which you're a member. Nothing.
- Attendance is more important to others than you imagine.
- Attendance is more critical for your growth than you imagine.

I remember my parents making church attendance a priority when we took trips. At the time I had no thought other than that we attend when the church meets. Period. I remember the first time I realized not every Christian family has the same mindset. I was around eight or nine years old, and a friend of mine, after telling me about her family's vacation to Disney World, said, "We didn't have to go to church because we weren't at home." It seemed strange at the time, but I've since thought about this and see the appeal to parents. They're on vacation. It should be a rest, and finding a place to worship and dragging kids to church is no rest.

Unfortunately, my friend's parents passed on a powerful message to their children: "You don't have to go to church all of the time. Disney World is more important." They would never have said this in so many words, but their actions said it loud and clear. Show your kids that nothing gets in the way of your regular worship.

When you set the example that attendance is nonnegotiable, the first thing your children will recognize is the importance of meeting with the other saints. When your children have grown, they'll have a more mature appreciation of what their participation means. Not only are they serving God, but they're also providing encouragement to others and learning for themselves.

If you've ever visited a very small congregation, you know how much the presence of visitors can uplift them. Don't be selfish on your vacations and keep your presence from a group who could use the encouragement. For graduate school, I went to a university located far from a faithful congregation. The other members and I drove about fifty minutes every Sunday and Wednesday night to get to the church building and another fifty minutes to get home. Habits from my childhood made this an easy task. The congregation had about fourteen members—including me. A newborn and I were the "kids." The newborn, a ninety-year-old man, and I were the "singles." We were a small group, and my presence and youth were valuable to them. Their presence was precious to me. I learned that attending worship is for God and the body of Christ.

You'll find that when you visit other congregations, your children will gain as much from that association as they are giving. My mom, sisters, and I went on a trip to Savannah, Georgia. We worshipped with the church there on a Sunday. It was a wonderful group. The thing that stood out to us was the work they were doing. After the worship service, they announced a list of other good works they would do in the coming week. The list never seemed to end. Those Christians were workers, and their community heard the gospel. Their example showed my family and me how much we aren't doing, and it's a lesson that has stuck with us.

Church attendance is just one example, but remember as a parent that your children will see all of the good you do. Do more, because they will also see the good you don't do.

Rosalind

A few years ago, over Christmas break, we got our dog, Judah. She was a tiny, bouncy puppy. Shortly afterward everyone went back to work, and I volunteered to babysit. It would be fun, right? She was my cute little pal. However, I quickly learned that underneath the fluffy exterior was a heart of mischief.

On one particular day, Judah woke up from napping, so I went to get her to carry her outside for a bathroom break. I got to her crate and saw that she had already had an accident. Not exactly exciting to see but also not a big deal, since she was a young puppy and house training takes months. I got her out, set her on the floor behind me, and began trying to clean out her crate. But she would not leave me alone. She was trying to push her way back into the crate, biting and scraping on everything in her path, severely testing my patience.

I knew I needed to put her somewhere while I cleaned, but she could not be left unsupervised, so I decided to put her in our empty jacuzzi tub. It seemed perfect, because I thought there was no way she could get out or cause any harm. Wrong. As soon as I set her down, she started licking the grunge that had accumulated around the jets. Terrified that she would get sick from the filth, I picked her up once again. She began flailing around in my arms and tore a hole in my sweater, a favorite sweater. I started crying.

An eight-pound, eight-week-old puppy brought me to tears—not tears of joy. However, my family members and I did not give up. Three years of discipline and training have given us the freedom to laugh at this story, because Judah has come so far. It is often the same with children. They start off small and cute and slowly begin to test your patience. They defy or ignore at times. They attempt things that are dangerous to their physical health and, as they grow, things that are dangerous to their spiritual health. Parents' ability to see the long view and imagine them as adults is key to being persistent when they are young and testing your endurance.

Much of the training I received as a child stuck with me because of repetition. In band we played songs repeatedly until we could play them with our eyes closed. I remember on one occasion we were practicing a song that had a tricky rest in it, meaning there was a moment during the song where everyone was supposed to be silent. We would play the song, and during the rest a clarinet, for example, would accidentally squeak out a note, and we had to start all over. Next time, another player committed the infraction. Over and over and over.

Each time we played with anticipation, waiting to see if everyone could be silent at the exact same moment. When the mistake happened again, the whole band groaned out loud, frustrated to start over another time. My band director had the forethought to know that if he let us give up after playing it once or twice with mistakes, we would botch it at the upcoming concert. Eventually, we played it perfectly.

When it comes to raising children, the goal is much more awe-inspiring than a successful band concert; it's a home in heaven. It is disheartening to enforce rules and guidelines repeatedly when your child continues to make the same mistakes. It would be a lot easier to just let it go. However, just like with the band, if you are persistent, kids will catch on, and when they are old, they will not depart from it (Proverbs 22:6).

Claire

Germany isn't a particularly religious country. I have just finished a semester of graduate school there as I write this. There are relatively few people who regularly attend church services. The church I met with was fairly humble, meeting in a room in an elementary school. Though many Germans outside the church rejected the idea of God and Jesus's sacrifice, the people of this congregation were unapologetic and open about wearing the name of Christ.

A high school student who had been attending church decided she would like to be baptized. She brought several friends from school to see her baptism. The baptism was in a bathtub. Nevertheless, she believed it was important for her secular friends to see this important step in her life. To her, church, school, and any other part of her life weren't kept separate. This is an area where it is easy to fall short. I have seen people who raised their children to work hard at a sport or play an instrument or succeed academically, which were very good things. However, these things were so heavily enforced that a compartment of the children's lives had to be neglected. That meant spirituality fell to the wayside.

It is human nature to be selfish and self-centered. When children never do anything for others or are not shown by parents that the world is not about them, they grow up to be this self-absorbed kind of people without realizing there is a better way. This is a trait we generally know and can spot in others, but can we home in on it in ourselves? Even if we are teaching our kids to be godly, have we taught them to be wise because of who they will be around in the world? Jesus says, "Behold, I send you out as sheep in the midst of wolves. Therefore be wise as serpents and harmless as doves" (Matthew 10:16). The warning is that wisdom is the armor of a saint in an environment ready to attack or at least recruit back to the world.

Assignments

1. Revisit the story about the high school parking lot fender bender, where the errant driver fled the scene and she and her father bore no responsibility. Think about what you would have done if you were the parent.
2. Answer and discuss with a partner the discussion questions below.
3. Continue to memorize Luke 4:1–14. Start wrapping up your memory work. But don't keep it to yourself—share it with someone.

Chapter 4 Discussion Questions

1. Discuss the challenges you have faced in "polishing" your child as she or he has grown. If you have more than one child, what particular differences did you find? When does the need for "polishing" stop?
2. Do you recall how early your parents began their training with you? How long did it last? Do you have a weak or strong quality of self-discipline as a result of this? Talk about the need for impressing on your child's mind at an early age the "can do" philosophy to promote self-discipline in him or her.
3. In the section on bad judgment, three considerations are given to help parents pay more attention to the consequences of their intervention or lack of it. They are as follows:
   - Mistakes and pain are valuable elements of learning.
   - The younger we are when we learn that our parents are right, the better.
   - Sisters and brothers learn valuable lessons from siblings' consequences.

   Discuss these in detail. What would you add to them?
4. We have noted that in the Bible, stones are a foundation—they represent something indestructible. Carry this thought over

to the Ken Kuykendall segment. Apply the biblical story of the wise man who built his house on the rock (Matthew 7:24–25) to this family. Ken's parents provided a solid foundation (the rock), Ken built his house on it, and the rains and floods and winds came. The result: "And it did not fall, for it was founded on the rock." We may never be faced with tragedies like these, but surely there will be tests. Discuss how critically important it is that we have an indestructible foundation for our faith to help us weather the storms in our lives.

5. Attendance at worship services is a vital part of establishing what God and His word mean to us. Discuss how you handle absences for vacations, school activities, etc. What priorities are you forming in your child for later years?
6. The story of training Judah when she was a puppy reinforces the need for repetition. "Polishing" can't be a hit-or-miss activity. Be persistent. What do you see as the greatest challenge in raising your children to be habitual in their spiritual service when they are "sheep in the midst of wolves"? List some ways you can help to instill in them their own faith in God as they grow up.

For Personal Use

Write down the most important concept you gained from chapter 4 in regard to developing spiritual tenacity in kids. You will be asked to do this for each chapter. Then personally review your answers at the conclusion of this twelve-lesson study. What did you learn about yourself? What can you pass on to the next generation? Hopefully, this will have been a profitable study for you.

5

WE, THE TEACHERS

Colleen

What would Jesus do? Teach. What does He do at the age of twelve? Teach—the temple teachers are amazed at His answers. What does He do just before His crucifixion? Teach. What does He do in His final forty days on this earth? Teach. If we profess to be His disciples, we had better be teaching. This must be learner-centered so that the focus is not first on what you will teach but on what your children or students will learn. They must learn capably and learn with vigor so that knowledge and wisdom are sturdy and ready for immediate action. Learning well is part of the groundwork on which perseverance is built.

A Life of Learning, Loyalty, and Leading

Joshua learned well. As we endeavor to teach our children, consider Joshua's learning that was the foundation of his determination. This warrior would have to rank in at least the Tenacity Top Ten of the Old Testament. In Numbers chapter 14, he, along with Caleb, has the steadfastness to hang onto rational thought even when everyone around him, including Moses and Aaron, is acting on emotion. Joshua and Caleb have just returned with the other ten spies from reconnaissance of the land of Canaan. There's an abundance of weeping and loud reaction as the ten spies bring intel of despair that Israel is up against an unbeatable foe. Joshua and Caleb verbally oppose a fever-pitched mob and speak optimistic words of the prized land and the strength and favor of God that will lead them.

Where did Joshua get that kind of moral stamina? He learned it. Learned it by seeing the great works of God in delivering Israel from Egyptian bondage (see Exodus 7–14). Learned it by the words of God, having been the only other person Moses took with him to receive the tablets of stone on Sinai. Each time Joshua walks by faith, this learning is reinforced, so that no one can shake his belief and courage. His life is spared in battle, and Israel is victorious against Amalek (Exodus 17:8–14). Joshua is rewarded for tenacity and faith as one of only two members of the older generation allowed to enter Canaan (Numbers 14:30).

God gives Joshua a way of life as plate armor in preparing Israel for the crossing of the Jordan into Canaan. He commands Joshua,

> Only be strong and very courageous, that you may observe to do according to all the law which Moses My servant commanded you; do not turn from it to the right hand or to the left, that you may prosper wherever you go. This Book of the Law shall not depart from your mouth, but you shall meditate in it day and night, that you may observe to do according to all that is written in it. For then you will make your way prosperous, and then you will have good success. Have I not commanded you? Be strong and of good courage; do not be afraid, nor be dismayed, for the LORD your God is with you wherever you go. (Joshua 1:7–9)

We know that Joshua does "meditate" and does "observe to do" and does "prosper," because the rest of the book of Joshua is the narrative of the conquest and settlement of Canaan under his leadership. At the end of his life, it is said that "Israel served the LORD all the days of Joshua, and all the days of the elders who outlived Joshua, who had known all the works of the LORD which He had done for Israel"

(24:31). He is unyielding to the end, and he leaves behind a faithful nation.

Joshua sees evidence and learns. He hears or reads the word of God and learns. He applies what he learns unwaveringly. Now transfer these aspects to instill learning in your own kids in spiritual and secular things starting, with three ideas:

1. Learning how to learn.
2. Being a super reader.
3. The daily gentle nudge.

Learning How to Learn

To bring new knowledge, behavior, and skills to a young one requires engagement of the mind and senses. To learn requires that a change has occurred in the learner. Learning happens just about anytime and anywhere. Learning may require a risk—a risk that you don't know everything or a risk of ego when you answer incorrectly. Some parents don't see themselves as teachers, and some children don't see themselves as students in any serious way. Learning can be tedious and focus elusive. Learning situations for kids are sometimes ineffective.

Newborns start learning immediately after delivery into this world. So begins the path to maturity. However, are children learning all that we think they are? Are they using what they learn? Are they sitting in seats while their minds are on the ball diamond? Have they learned merely how to appear attentive? Well, maybe they get the answers correct, but the content is undemanding and the standard so low that they can daydream in class and still pass the test.

What we want for our children is for them to be very good at learning. The sooner, the quicker, and the more they learn, the better. Now, this must be tailored for each child, which requires knowing the child's abilities well. Also, proficiency trumps timeliness and speed in most cases. Unfortunately, variables can block learning so that the process is ineffective. Consider a few potential blocks, along with ways you can counter them:

1. The child isn't interested in the subject or teacher, so the mind and senses aren't engaged. Think about it; much of what kids learn in school and in other venues is very important in the long run but not urgently relevant to their little minds now. Multiplication tables, World War II, and molecules don't matter to children in any tangible way just yet. That's why it is difficult to stay engaged with this crucial learning content. What's on the lunch menu and that their cousin is visiting are relevant to children. Whenever possible, think ahead and find a way to apply the lesson to what matters to them. I can teach my students all day long about forgiving enemies. We can read it in our Bibles, and they can answer questions. But do you know when the lightbulb flashes on? It's when I tell them their enemy may just be in their own house. "Does your brother ever tease you or play a trick on you and laugh?" I ask. Yes, they all have a story. It's now relevant.
2. The child is afraid to fail at acquiring new knowledge or skills and therefore disengages. This may wax worse as children become older and are more self-conscious. When teaching kids, try to neutralize the fear factor by outlawing comments or snickers from the other kids or siblings, and make a steep penalty for noncompliance. For instance, if a child can't think of an answer in a game and another child laughs or says, "That's easy," the culprit has to miss his or her turn. It works. Be careful how you react as well. I also have the students listen to me recite the assigned memory work and correct me if I flub. This sends an important message that we're all learning and making mistakes, even the adults. So what?
3. The parent or teacher is intimidating or boring and therefore alienates the students. When I was a new driver, I was excited at the opportunity to learn to drive a manual-shift car. An adult took me out on the road for my lesson, telling me each step in the process. Of course, I was grinding and stalling and becoming more exasperated by the minute. My teacher sputtered

commands and corrections at me as both our anxiety levels skyrocketed. After lesson one we parted, never to reunite for lesson two. I don't know how to drive a stick shift. I can live without that skill, but the real damage is that I didn't want that person to teach me anything else, and I suspect that with each learning failure, I became more and more picky about what I was willing to try. It's not natural, but it is essential that teachers and parents stay calm and responsive through the stress of learning. The stakes are very high, as the sixteen-year-old in me can tell you decades later.

4. Too many or too few kids in the learning situation spoils the dynamics. In some situations my kids had success in learning one-on-one with the teacher; for instance, with musical instrument lessons. However, being part of a large group of kids who traveled abroad was also a favorable learning environment. The point is that you'll have to think of this variable ahead of time and try to calculate if and how class numbers will affect the learning.
5. Teachers and parents aren't wise to the wiles of children. Learning requires effort, so at least some children will spend more energy devising ways to avoid it than if they had just done the work. With some children, if I ask them if they want to lead a prayer in Bible class, they say, "No." If I tell them to lead the prayer, they just do it. For memorizing scripture, I've had kids deliberately fail to do it for several weeks. I'm pretty sure they're thinking I will give up and move on to the next scheduled memory verse. I don't let them play me that way.
6. Learning tasks can be tedious and boring. In this case be creative, and think of ways to take out the tedium. For instance, offer a reward of something fun when the children finish the boring work. Also, having Mom, Dad, or a sibling around for the learning task can mitigate the dullness. One time I challenged my girls to memorize a whole chapter of scripture. I got a lot less resistance by accomplishing it with them. Also, my kids

didn't like to practice the piano, so sometimes I would just sit in the room and work on my own business while they practiced. It seemed to make the situation more tolerable for them.

7. Focus is elusive. Perhaps this is one of the main culprits that steal productivity in the classroom. It's difficult to concentrate, especially on something that's not relevant to us. One method that may help with this is to eliminate distractions. Also, to become adept at reading forces the mind to process text into a cohesive narrative. One must concentrate to absorb the information and keep it relevant to the overall story. Developing analytical skills pays off. When my daughters started college, I asked the dean to rank each discipline in the business school by expected salary. Each time his answer was the same. As he ranked them, he explained that the more analytical the major, the higher the pay. Analyzing business data affects earnings on Earth. Analyzing the word of God brings spiritual gain. The capacity to focus mental energy on the learning task is decisive in a child's progress.

Many of these blocks to learning can be surmounted if forethought is employed and strategies adjusted. As with Joshua, knowledge and experience will undergird our fortitude to stay strong spiritually and in life's jobs. We must unshackle our children so that they learn with a potency that applies lessons in a well-rounded way.

Being a Super Reader

Reading text is the next best thing to reading someone's mind. It's fairly cheap and simple. Joshua learns by reading and hearing the word of God. It is his meditation. That's how it stays fresh in the minds and hearts of God's people. That God commands Joshua to read the law and meditate implies that it's something he'll have to do intentionally; it doesn't just happen.

Christianity is a text-based course. Like Joshua, if we want our children to learn, let the information bloom in their minds, and keep it from perishing, they must sustain the reading and digesting. Reading is an imperative skill in knowing God and also in acquiring information needed to navigate life in general. In contrast, not being an impeccable reader is spiritually and secularly precarious indeed.

Being a super reader means developing your reading muscles. Have you ever read the Bible or some other book or document and found that when you've finished a passage, you can't recall anything you read? With perplexity, people mention this problem to me sometimes. It's not a phenomenon; it's most likely not a learning disability or sign of mental decline. It's flabby reading muscles. The brain is on autopilot, allowing the reader to recognize the words and dismiss their import while concentrating on something else. Or how about when you really do focus on a text but are frustrated because you don't easily comprehend? Flabby reading muscles.

I know about this malady because my reading muscles have been out of condition, then bulked up, and are now slipping back to sagginess again as I write. When I was in graduate school and reading many books—textbooks, Victorian novels, and literary criticism—it was labor but to considerable gain. I first had to make myself focus and digest to keep from getting to the bottom of the page with no earthly idea what I'd just read. I couldn't waste time like that. To fix this problem, I forced myself to go back and read; no moving on without comprehension. No cheat. If you teach your kids to faithfully give themselves that little consequence, their reading muscles will get into shape pronto. They don't want to have to reread, so they pay attention the first time.

For the difficult readings, like some poetry or literary criticism written for geniuses by geniuses, ordinary focus wasn't enough for me. I had to read passages repeatedly until I understood, analogous to the way one builds up arm muscles to lift heavier weights. It's grueling and not pleasant, but it augments the mind for deeper meanings. Use what I learned from my pain to build true reading power in your kids and yourselves.

My poor kids were in public school when I was doing hard labor with the books, so I applied the principles to their situations.

They usually had a book going. I carefully chose most of them. While the girls had to read what was assigned in school, I also handed out my choices. I believe it was when one of my daughters was in eighth grade and part of an accelerated class that I noticed the assigned book was written on a third-grade level. Reading below grade level doesn't build reading muscles any more than playing a game of basketball against a younger child increases athletic skill.

Hawthorne, Alcott, Twain, the Brontës—classics were a must. My main goal was that the girls would develop their brains to comprehend and use the lofty thoughts and plots to think deeply. I didn't worry much about whether they liked the books, any more than a parent getting his kids in shape for a sport asks if they like leg squats. If they stay with the reading and the leg squats long enough, there will arise huge dividends. After tackling something like, say, Dickens, my kids were allowed to read an easy kid detective novel for a reward.

Most importantly, the Bible should be everyday required reading. If your kids are still at home or if you have nieces, nephews, or grandchildren, read the Bible with them daily. I don't feel like I did it enough. It is easy to read the Bible and just as easy to neglect.

The Daily Gentle Nudge

Fortunately for our purposes, among those who have not yet obeyed the gospel of Jesus Christ, children are the most agreeable, influenceable lot you can find. The gospel is the most practical, optimistic, and user-friendly message you could teach—it's the good news of salvation and eternal life in heaven. Since we have an eager audience and a foolproof message, the ways and means are endless and at hand. Deuteronomy 6:7 regulates the time and physical positions for Israel to teach the Law of Moses, which are anytime and any pose: "You shall teach them diligently to your children, and shall talk of them when you sit in your house, when you walk by the way, when you lie down, and when you rise up." Of particular focus in this passage are the girls and boys who are learning. Seize all opportunities to pass God's word to them when they're under your roof and impressionable.

Similar exhortations for Christians to live by appear in the New Testament. The apostle Paul, in Ephesians 6:4, emphasizes instructing your children instead of exasperating them when he writes, "And you, fathers, do not provoke your children to wrath, but bring them up in the training and admonition of the Lord." Now I'm sure my kids weren't the first to try to get out of a directive by alleging, "He's provoking me to wrath," when their dad told them to do some loathed chore. At least they could quote scripture, but they mangled the point. Parents can easily frustrate children by either directing them to perform an unfair task or by delivering the order in a manner that incurs anger. Instead we should admonish or train with that admonition wrapped in a blanket of nurture and protective encouragement.

The best way I know to achieve this training mojo is to execute the verbal training with nurture on a daily, even hourly basis. Inconsistency is the taunter of training efforts. For example, if your child is left to his own devices when it comes to completing Bible class work, then it's unreasonable to expect him to suddenly be disciplined in preparing for class. If you find out he is not doing the classwork, blowing up at him only provokes wrath, because while he knows how to fill out the lesson sheet and memorize scripture, you haven't conditioned him to carry out those tasks. You first must condition yourself to train him with a daily gentle nudge.

If your children watch television or something fun while you set the table and prepare meals on a regular basis, then it's unfair to expect them to suddenly be skilled at and habituated to helping with a big gathering such as Thanksgiving. Yes, they may know how to perform some of the tasks associated with the meal, but that's only part of the recipe. Another part is being in the habit of accepting the tasks as routine. One other aspect is having enough experience with the tasks to carry them out with confidence. Stressed out parents snapping orders in the kitchen now provoke wrath, because they're on edge and asking for performance that is not required all year. The solution is a daily gentle nudge. Consistency. Plus thinking ahead.

Sometimes parents (including me) give a new instruction and then duck out of sight, only to resurface in exasperation later. For instance, let's say a parent decides the kids' bedrooms are disgracefully messy and makes a rule that no items can be thrown on the floor or bed. Then the parent walks away for two weeks without reminders or inspections. The next time the parent happens into one of the bedrooms, she's vexed because she sees the same old chaos. The solution here is also the daily gentle nudge.

Yes, make the mandates, but on a regular basis ask about progress with the Bible worksheet and memory verse. If necessary, come up with a strategy such as designating a special place to keep the Bible notebook and Bible. Schedule a particular time to complete Bible classwork. Get everybody into the habit of setting the table and helping in the kitchen every day of the year so that holiday entertaining looks like a Norman Rockwell painting. Remember your rule about no items on the bedroom floor and then follow through. Take a peek every day or so and give a pat on the back or some pressure to help them remember the rule. The key is that you have to follow through. The most obedient kids in the world will imitate your example, even if it's a bad one. If you let your rules languish, they will let them languish too.

The Daily Gentle Nudge toward God

Nowhere is that daily gentle nudge more important than in children's spiritual training. So much has to be explained for boys and girls, especially when teaching the Bible. It's an ancient Eastern book. Much of what's discussed can be understood by children but requires extensive clarification. That's why I run out of time when teaching kids' Bible classes. I have to explain what taxes are, and tax collectors, incense, wolves in sheep's clothing, and so on.

Half the effort is helping children to understand the Bible plot. You must set yourself up as the teacher from day one. Ezra, Nehemiah, and the Levites got face-to-face with the people to establish the teaching relationship, and we have got to do the same. Don't hand off your responsibility to other people. Make yourself a tough act to follow, not a tough act to find.

Haley

Jean-Jacques Rousseau—the famed philosopher—studied the art of pedagogy. In the book *Emile*, he details what he perceives to be the best methods of raising children who are strong of body and mind. Having observed a lazy child, he writes, "Somehow or other he had got it into his head that a man of his rank need know nothing and do nothing—that his birth would serve as a substitute for arms and legs, as well as for every kind of virtue" (Rousseau 2013, 191). This child did not have the desire to learn, having discovered that his mere existence made him worthy of inaction. I daresay that his outlook was cultivated to some degree by the example of his parents. The sad part and what all of us see is that a child who is allowed to continue in this view will be a weak adult.

You Learn, They Learn

If you're a parent who doesn't know how or care to learn, I wouldn't expect your children to value learning. On the other hand, if you're a parent who takes time and effort to sharpen your mind and broaden your understanding, your children are well on their way to becoming far-above-average adults.

Rousseau's lazy child sees no value in improving himself because he is somehow above the work necessary for development. But children are natural learners. They are curious and love to put new things into their brains, so how could this be? That's all true of children unless someone shows them another way. If, for instance, a parent doesn't take time to learn or read, a child will put her resources to more valued tasks.

Will your children see you reading your Bible today? If they see you watching television instead, don't be surprised if they grow up valuing television over the study of God's word. Will they see you invite anyone to hear the gospel preached? If you're always too tired for inviting, don't be surprised if your children never find the time for it either. As much as you may tell them reading the Bible and spreading the Word is essential, your words are only as useful as the actions that back them up.

I worshipped with a congregation with several families and lots of children. Usually the preacher taught the adult Bible class, but in one semester he taught the middle school class instead. He was appalled when he realized that the students in the class never did the expected preparation before Bible class. Now, I have no doubt the parents of these kids told them to do their lessons, but it wasn't translating. The preacher's response was to compel the parents to do their own Bible lessons. After that there was no problem with under preparedness in the middle school class. Remember the lazy child from Rousseau. You'd never want yours to end up that way, so prove that what you say is important enough for you to carry out.

You may not have chosen a career of teaching, but by right of being humans, we are all required to be teachers. Maybe you haven't had formal training in education, but your job to teach remains the same. Luckily, one of the simplest—though maybe not easiest—ways of teaching is also one of the most effective. Parents, you must do as you teach.

Rosalind

Lessons from Teachers: Good and Bad

Who was your favorite teacher as a child? Your least favorite? Think about the differences between the two. For me, the favorite teachers obviously loved the subject and went to great lengths to foster that same love in their students. Have you ever found yourself on the edge of your seat, listening to a speaker discuss a topic you were never before interested in? Teachers have the ability to spark interest and enjoyment in difficult subjects and many times can be the reason for a student's success instead of failure.

Part of my required undergraduate coursework included a class on individual taxes. I spent an entire semester studying one of the most dreaded topics known to Americans. It sounds miserable, but I actually came to enjoy the class. Many would rather watch paint dry than practice completing tax returns, but my professor was able to take a dull subject and make it quite fun. The class was interactive, and we were encouraged to learn as opposed to just pass an exam. The activities were engaging, and our professor kept the classroom environment light and pleasant. The taxation course could have easily been one where snoring was regularly heard from the back row; instead students were immersed and learning with enthusiasm.

Children's Deep Sense of Fairness

As a student I felt frustrated toward teachers and other adults who were inconsistent or unfair in their behavior. Teaching certainly is a test of patience, especially when your students are children. But children are humans too, and they are very likely to remember your behavior, good or bad.

For example, on one particular school day, I entered the band room and prepared for practice. I sat at my chair and put my school books in the wire rack attached to the bottom of my seat. Everyone around me was getting situated as well. The band director stepped up to the front and got our attention for practice to begin. He called out a song, everyone got quiet in preparation, and the director raised his hands to signal the start. Just as that happened, the books under my chair fell out onto the floor, so I leaned over to pick them up and place them back on the rack. As I was picking up the books, I noticed that the band had not yet started to play, and it was quiet until I heard, "Ms. O'Steen, are you going to join the rest of us?"

I leaned up, terrified, and tried to explain what happened. Instead of meeting listening with the intention of understanding, I was told to meet my director in his office after practice, the sentence for misbehaving band kids, not exactly my crowd. After practice I once again tried to explain that I had done nothing wrong, but in return I was told that I was a disappointment.

I rarely ever got into trouble at school, so this infuriated and embarrassed me. I knew I had done nothing worthy of disappointment, but my teacher chose to tell me otherwise, and it stuck with me. This story is a useful reminder to me that anytime I am a teacher, I need to dedicate myself to seeking fairness at all times. Students, definitely young ones, notice when things are unjust. "That's not fair!" As a child I said this more times than I can remember.

A friend of mine has a couple of children who go to summer camps every year. Her children have an aversion to one camp in particular. The camp's reasoning is this: if one kid breaks the rules, everyone has to sit out. The well-behaved children can easily see that there is no logic in this.

Most importantly, when it comes to teaching souls about Christ, it is imperative to know how to avoid discouraging students or alienating them, because our God wants all souls to be saved and know His truth (see 1 Timothy 2:4). What does the Lord require of us, even as teachers? "To do justly, to love mercy, and to walk humbly with your God" (Micah 6:8).

Claire

Bible class teachers operate as some of that grit in the rock tumbler. However, we can become far removed from being a child and forget that there are different approaches to teaching—some successful for retention, some not. A main goal of Bible class is for students to know God, but sometimes this goal is crowded by other factors.

When I first began teaching Bible class, of course I was inexperienced, but I was in public high school then and sitting through a few boring classes with teachers who weren't enthused about their jobs. I was not far from being the age of the students I was teaching in Bible class and understood that recall of information wouldn't happen unless something occurred during the lessons that was worth paying attention to. That led me to really contemplate the following reflection: "I remember many concepts and stories from Bible class, but I have few memories of doing things in Bible class. How can I make my class meaningful enough for these kids to remember when they're my age?"

One important reason for the kids to retain specific learning methods and activities is that this gives them a memorable foundation for when they begin to teach their own Bible classes. It led me to do things like letting the students act as the Israelites looking for the culprit who stole booty and caused defeat at Ai in Joshua 7. I divided them until we got to "Achan" and then explored his tent to find the stolen goods. I had set up my tent in an empty classroom and hidden a garment and "precious metals" inside.

We tasted honey to use our senses in understanding John the Baptist's diet and various passages in the Bible. We did a Bible relay to test students' retention of class material and their readiness in flipping to passages in the Bible. It took a lot of time—I could spend many hours preparing for just one lesson. Part of the difficulty was the balance and constraint of time. In being the grit for students, I used mental determination to refine how I executed my role in teaching.

Learning from Everyday Examples

When I moved to Germany last year for a semester of graduate school, I contacted some Christians in Hamburg and just showed up at church services. There was one particular couple (in addition to other Christians) at church who really looked out for me. What an example of unselfishness and true discipleship they were.

When my friends at school saw me bring home food sent by Heide and Harry, they were shocked by the hospitality of these people who were virtual strangers. They were ever so much more shocked when they heard the couple had given me a very nice bike to use. For those students, bestowing something of value on a stranger was a foreign (no pun intended) concept. It wasn't foreign to Heide, Harry, and me as Christians. Several months later the bike was stolen. With as much grace as they had given the bike, they forgave the matter. This was another thing that put my friends in awe, saying, "We ought to start going to church!"

Perhaps my friends hadn't experienced this kind of service in their upbringing. I plan to one day teach my children what it means to be selfless by doing a few things I have noticed that seem to work, providing an example of giving something I'd like to keep so that another can have something she needs. In the future I want to give my children opportunities to demonstrate this, taking them to visit the elderly or sick to see it's not all about me. I can learn from the wisdom of others, instilling the importance of writing thank you notes to show appreciation for and to acknowledge the sacrifice someone else has made for me. I'm not many years from the heart of the child, and it informs me as I plan ways to prepare kids for maturity in Christ.

Assignments

1. Answer and discuss with a partner or class the questions below.
2. Recite Luke 4:1–14 from memory. How far can you get without a mistake? Keep working on it. Memorizing a long passage takes a lot of practice but will yield big returns as it stays planted in your mind.
3. Remember the assignment from chapter 2 to develop a new habit that takes self-discipline and requires that you follow through indefinitely? Whether or not you are continuing faithfully in that new habit can be a useful projection of how you will fare in following through when leading the younger generation.

Chapter 5 Discussion Questions

1. Reread God's commands to Joshua (1:7–9). Do you want your child to be prosperous and have good success? What are the vital actions you must do to achieve this end? How will God be with us as we follow His precepts?
2. This section presents seven blocks to learning. Review them individually. Have you encountered any (or all) of these? How can you effectively use the suggestions offered to produce the objective of a change in the learner?
3. How important is it that your child become a "super reader"? Do you start each day with a Bible reading? (It will get your and your child's day off right.) Do you ask your child to explain the passage? How is this important for her or his understanding? Is this also necessary for secular reading? There is no occupation that does not require comprehensive reading skills—even cleaning house demands that you be able to read directions on the products you use.
4. Every day presents new opportunities to pass God's word to your children. Describe some scenarios throughout your day

(cf. Deuteronomy 6:7) when you could reinforce God's commands by gentle nudges.

5. Children are natural learners. What do you see as your greatest responsibility in directing how and what they learn? How important is your example in this process?
6. What can we learn from Rosalind's course on tax return preparation to apply to making the learning process more palatable for our kids? Describe some ways in which you have done this.
7. Have you used some of the teaching methods described by Claire? What success did you have? Do you agree that Bible stories become more real to students who actively participate in the telling?

For Personal Use

Write down the most important concept you gained from chapter 5 in regard to developing spiritual courage in kids. You will be asked to do this for each chapter. Then personally review your answers at the conclusion of this twelve-lesson study. Have these important concepts changed you? How will you extend them to younger people?

6

YO, HEAVE HO: WORK ETHIC

Colleen

That work is intrinsic to the existence of human beings is exemplified by the fact that God creates it before He creates them. In Genesis chapter 1, the abundance of sea creatures, the various plants, and the fruitful multiplication of birds and beasts provide the raw material for fulfilling God's command to "have dominion over the fish of the sea, over the birds of the air, and over every living thing that moves on the earth" (v. 28). Work has been a part of God's plan for the world since the beginning. People have labored to survive, for glory, out of boredom, by oppression, and to get rich. One thing's for sure: there is always more work to do.

Toil is a sustained theme of the Bible, from the Genesis perspiration to the Gospels' Great Commission, all the way to Revelation's reward. It reads, "Blessed are those who do His commandments, that they may have the right to the tree of life, and may enter through the gates into the city" (Revelation 22:14). The apostle Paul tells the Thessalonian Christians to "lead a quiet life, to mind your own business, and to work with your own hands, as we commanded you, that you may walk properly toward those who are outside, and that you may lack nothing" (1 Thessalonians 4:11–12). We are to be attentive to our Father's business and work at earthly tasks that provide for physical needs. The hitch is that we must be self-starters when it comes to carrying out God's commands and earning a living.

Work from the Cradle

It is that motivated mind that can build a child's very core from birth. It nourishes a spiritual staying power for assessing needs, getting work done, and solving problems one way or another. The opposite is children who grow better and better at getting out of labor, who spend more time and effort wiggling out of chores and school tasks than if they'd just complied with the assignments.

Work is effort or exertion that leads to a finished product or reward of some sort. Ethic is your personal rules of conduct or those followed by a group. Put them together and you have work ethic: one's personal approach to getting things done.

There are bits of this concept that all of us like; there are prospects we don't want. Work can appear glamorous or gratifying from a distance; it can be boring, sweaty, painful, and a whole lot of other objectionable adjectives close up. Having grown up on a farm in the Midwest, keeping house for a family of five, and managing a career of nearly forty years, I can tell you that no other trait will win the esteem or disdain of others faster than the quality of your work ethic. It is a major factor in determining how productive you are in supplying your own needs, and it also affects what you add to the production of others and whether they have to shore up your rickety efforts.

A worker can be good-looking, charming, and impressive with the job skills, but if he or she is late, lazy, or lacking in contributions to the work, colleagues learn to loathe and ridicule that colleague. I know of two cases where a person made an excuse for being late or for not being able to work overtime. The excuses probably sounded plausible to them, but for years—in one case, more than a decade—coworkers have made fun of them behind their backs. On the flip side, a person can be unbathed and boorish, but if she or he is a hard worker and a true-blue team player, colleagues will probably overlook the personality flaws and the body odor.

I can't imagine any parents planning for their children to evolve into idle and unproductive adults. However, we can make decisions today that default to their idleness and dependency on others in the future. If we don't know kids and ourselves very well, we can inadvertently help them grow up to be excuse makers and a laughingstock, not to mention empty in the billfold. To avoid this parents must develop a serious work ethic—spiritual and otherwise—in their children from the beginning.

The Song of the Volga Boatmen

My expertise in the realm of work ethic goes back decades and is not praiseworthy. In some ways it is related to the chant, "Yo, heave ho." As a child I loathed taking piano lessons and the practice that went with them. One of my primary books featured what I saw as the creepy "Song of the Volga Boatmen" about laborers pulling a barge. It was a Russian work song in a minor key, and I felt the doom with each chord. "Yo, heave ho!" was the refrain of the men toiling under the load.

Always ready to dodge anything tedious or without immediate ample reward, I once got my sister to "Yo, heave ho" her way through my piano practice. We shut the door to the piano room, and for all Mom knew, I was the one practicing. I also would "forget" my piano books when I went to my lesson. That was just the beginning of my shiftless work ethic, but you get the picture. I grew up, realized I had short-changed myself in a distressing way, and was ready to make it right for my children. I do know something about putting the kibosh on kids' efforts to slither away from work.

Don't Fall for This Myth

The myth is that other kids are naturally smart, hard workers, well-behaved, organized, and so on. I fell for this myth growing up. I have seen parents and other children do the same. I can't think of a falsehood that does more damage to a child's potential than this easy-to-fall-for illusion. If children are smart, hardworking, well-behaved, and organized, mostly likely their parents are managing them to perform that way. IQ, natural inclination, and so on play a role, but who wouldn't want their children to reach their full potential, whatever that is? Our kids struggled with some subjects, but instead of giving them a pass, we told them they would have to work extra diligently to master them.

At least for my kids and me, in order to achieve things, we had to do a lot of work that doesn't pay off. Children are motivated by instantaneous reward or punishment. It's difficult for them to do something they don't want to do when the reward or punishment may never materialize or, if it does, may take a long time. The truth is that working for the one thing that you like that will bring big rewards is an immature plan that affords little productivity. What if it doesn't work out?

Having a strong work ethic that covers all areas all the time will bring some rewards. Playing their on game, strong game 24/7 develops self-discipline in children so that it doesn't feel like work but just the way they operate. For instance, if kids are respectful and friendly to everyone, they won't have time to be disappointed when a favorite friend slights them. There are plenty of other friends to focus on. If kids regularly read their Bibles, pray, help the needy, and generally attend to the Father's business, they will see in time that it doesn't matter whether anyone noticed or they got points in a game for knowing something.

Vacuuming

When kids first learn to vacuum the floors, they see some dirt, walk over, and suck it up. They see a dust bunny and suck it up. You have to correct this and teach them that there's a whole lot of trash and dirt they don't see, so they must vacuum every inch of the floor to make sure even the unseen anomalies meet their doom. For a long time, I thought that was all you needed to know about vacuuming, but I was wrong.

The last time we had new carpet installed in our house, I was curious to learn how to preserve it. The carpet installers and a woman who cleans professionally pointed out that there's microscopic dirt that sticks the fibers together each time someone steps on them, sending the carpet toward a grungy appearance and a gradual decline. To solve this problem, they told me to vacuum every day to manage that issue and protect my investment.

Apply this to your work ethic and that of your kids, going from a shallow, immature viewpoint to a committed frame of mind that's set on a long perspective of time. Just like with vacuuming, you won't get the best results if you practice a quality work ethic only once per week. Don't let those in the next generation settle for giving short shrift. Insist on a mature job in whatever is before them. If they don't do it the way you want them to, have them do it again correctly. I remember my dad making me get the vacuum cleaner back out and do the job again because I had missed so much the first time. He also gave me nasty, gross jobs to do, like cleaning out a shed that mice had been living in. Stinky, unpleasant jobs can be character building. If nothing else, we learn we don't want them as a career.

I know someone with a child who has learning disabilities. She told him to sweep the deck. He was doing it—sort of. He was making a swinging motion but wasn't holding the broom correctly and certainly wasn't making much contact with the dirty deck. Some parents would rationalize that it is easier to leave him alone, but she was willing to do the work of making him hold the broom the right way and not letting him off the hook. If you are committed to developing a solid work ethic in your children, get ready for your own work ethic to ratchet up a few notches. You will be tired. They will learn. Your work ethic will now be theirs.

Practical Tips for Driving an Admirable Work Ethic

The following is a list of ideas to help you move from theory to practice in the day-to-day business of instilling good work attitudes and actions in your children and students.

1. Allowance or not? My husband and I wanted our kids to have some money to manage but also felt that they should work diligently without pay. Here is our solution. They did work

around the house for free, carrying out whatever was assigned. We also gave them a few chores to complete for their allowance, a small amount per week, starting at around $5 and going up to around $15 as they got older. To earn the allowance, they had to do the chores correctly and without being reminded. If they were reminded, they didn't get the money and had to do the chores anyway. Occasionally, if I had a big job, like washing the car, I would pay them only if they had already earned their allowance. It taught them to be self-starters and gave them money to save, spend, and donate.

2. We chose not to have a riding lawnmower. Instead, my husband refurbished old push mowers for the task. He and all three girls would go at it together, mowing our large lawn. This taught them the joy of physical labor, that simpler is often better, and that their parents work too. Of course, they now know how to cut grass with expertise.
3. Let your kids see you doing work. It's often easier to get the work done without children and others distracting you, but an example is only useful if it is observable. I knew a Christian who often studied his Bible, but he realized that his kids did not see him because he was in another room or they weren't around. He changed his habit and started studying his Bible out in the open to let his light shine.
4. Keep it fresh. Novelty is a shallow factor that attracts humans to things. Kids are naturally drawn to activities because they're new. Eventually the newness wears off and their passion flags. That's when parents must add fresh dimensions to the activity and be creative in order to continue the energy for that activity or pursuit. When I was in middle school band, my mom bought me a book of trumpet arrangements of The Carpenters' songs. Getting me out of the standard band book pieces motivated me to practice.
5. Returning to my mantra, a gentle nudge or monitoring every day or every other day is the way to get young ones to

accomplish something monumental and complicated. Don't just command and walk away from it for a month only to return disappointed.

6. Make it manageable. When students have a big project, cut it up into phases and give it a schedule so that each part is small and not overwhelming. Let them have the satisfaction of crossing off each task as it is fulfilled.
7. Set a deadline. It's not a magic wand, but it adds reality to a tedious pile of procrastination.

Work Ethic Is Self-Policing

Of course, the ultimate goal is for children to move from being guided by adults to being self-starters. At the heart of this is the ability to analyze priorities, motives, and actions objectively in relation to their loyalty to God. I use little tricks to keep myself and others honest in this way. One is what I'll call the money test. Here's how it played out one time. It was almost the end of the year in my third grade Bible class, and a little girl was behind on memorizing two pieces of scripture. She chose not to get the work done until time was running out. Then she told me she was going on vacation and might not have time to learn her memory verses at all.

I suggested that vacations are the perfect time to memorize scripture because of all the hours that can be used to learn while riding in a car or plane. A week or so later, she returned with the bad news that she hadn't learned her memory verses. I asked, "If I had told you that if you learned them by the time you got back that I would give you five hundred dollars, would you have learned them?" She gave me a wry smile and a half nod that told me I had her.

Did I have you? I had me too. It's so much easier to exert myself when I know the reward is tangible, worth it, and soon. That's the stumbling block with much of our work of consequence—the reward is far in the distance, or someone else feels the true benefits. Think of the long list of tasks you perform in the kingdom of God to show your love for Him and your neighbor. Much of that doesn't pay a physical or emotional reward, unless you've trained yourself to feel one. It doesn't pay the way five hundred dollars for reciting a piece of scripture would. Think of all you sacrifice for your kids, your spouse, the unsaved, the community, and the underprivileged. Getting your children to do what should be done, at the right time and whether or not their heart is in it, is key in imitating your quality work ethic. The money test helps us all self-police.

Haley

One of the most difficult things about being a Christian is that the job is never finished. There's no end point on this earth when we can take a vacation before starting a new project. There are no breaks. This work we do is constant. Having the mindset to face the work for decades increases the likelihood that one is separated with the wheat instead of the chaff on the judgment day.

The hope is that your child's heart will be good soil in which the word sprouts and flourishes. In the parable in Matthew 13, the sower's seed that lands on fertile ground produces vast crops, and you want your children to produce one hundred, sixty, or thirty times more than what you plant. But anybody who has a vague notion of how plants grow knows that farmers or gardeners don't leave planting to chance. A good parent doesn't just hope that what she teaches falls on good ground. Cultivate and fertilize children's hearts so that the eternal outcome for them will be sure reward.

A parent's job is to equip his or her child to do the work God requires of a Christian. I believe equipping means more than teaching them what the Bible says and hoping they have a heart of good soil. It requires tending and cultivating—backbreaking labor. An important way to cultivate your children's hearts is to teach them to be perseverant. God doesn't ask us to do difficult things, but the things He asks of us are for a lifetime. That means your children don't need to be the best or highest achieving at everything, but they do need the ability to keep on keeping on.

Obtaining the kingdom of heaven is something like getting a PhD. When I was working on my degree, I realized quickly that people who get doctoral degrees are not necessarily the smartest, but they are willing to work consistently for four, maybe five years or more. The people who drop out are as smart as the ones who stay in, but they don't want to do the work anymore. My advisor said, "The students who don't make it through the program are the ones who do a lot of cleaning." And he was right. One student who was gone after the first year, the hardest year, of our program told me about his studying the night before an exam. He had dusted the tops of his cabinets. He'd never dusted before in his life, but when schoolwork needed to be done, any other activity was preferred. Even though he wanted to see the result of having the degree, he didn't want to do the years of work it would take to get it.

Everyone wants to see eternal reward, but most can't stomach the years of work required. To develop your children's hearts into good soil, teach them to persevere. That's what it takes to get to heaven.

They'll need your example. Show them that you work hard. If they see you come home from your job and sit down in front of the TV, they only see you watch the screen—not the eight hours of work that came before. That means parents must make a conscious effort to work in front of their kids to show them that being a responsible person and a Christian requires being uncomfortable.

Your children also need your guidance. Don't just show them that you work. Give them practice at working and working and working some more. It's one thing for a child to understand that it's good to do hard work and persevere, but it's another for her to know she can and must resist temptation in order to complete the work. Be an example of perseverance and make your kids practice that often unappreciated virtue. You'll have given them a great gift that helps them on their way to heaven.

Rosalind

At my grandfather's funeral, the speaker read Colossians 3:23-24, which states, "And whatever you do, do it heartily, as to the Lord and not to men, knowing that from the Lord you will receive the reward of the inheritance; for you serve the Lord Christ." It was obvious to the speaker and to everyone who knew him that my grandfather lived a life full of hard, dedicated work, start to finish. He was a child during the Great Depression, served our country in World War II, was a successful businessman, and raised five children, among other things. After the funeral I was so inspired by his work ethic that I framed the Colossians verse and displayed it in my home as a daily reminder to work hard at everything I do. From the simplest everyday chore to a daunting, seemingly never-ending task, God has asked us to do it wholeheartedly.

My mom advises to break up large projects into smaller, more manageable ones, as well as to set deadlines, and I could not agree more. Even if the work ahead of me is something I am passionate about, big projects can feel overwhelming. The feeling of not knowing where to begin to complete a huge task contributes to losing a strong work ethic. Maybe your child has a Bible class assignment more challenging than ever before. Teach your student to separate the task into sections, set dates that each section has to be done, and stick to it. Have you ever planned a wedding? It is likely one of the most joyful events of your life but also a task that can cause a lot of stress. But breaking down the planning into smaller goals relieves pressure and prepares you to be a solid worker. I rely on deadlines at work on a regular basis. Not only do they keep me on track, but they also keep my team members aligned with me.

One of the most imperative parts of becoming a hard worker, or raising one, is devotion to the correcting of mistakes and striving for continuous improvement. I remember an elementary school teacher of mine reviewing handwriting assignments and sending several children back to recomplete the task, saying the writing looked like "chicken scratch." It seemed like a harsh criticism at the time to such young children, but it was a necessary one that prevented kids from growing up and having the type of handwriting that other people have to squint at and guess about the message. It's not fun being the one who is always pointing out or correcting mistakes—it can be quite exhausting—but time is saved in the long run. You, your children, your employees, or whoever is a worker-in-training will build that strong work ethic mentioned in Colossians and come to need less guidance.

Claire

At first, push-mowing the lawn was fun. Then it got difficult. One thing that made the hard work more bearable was when my parents or sisters mowed with me. Now I know I can crank my own mower. I know to go around the edge of the grass several times, with the grass blowing inside so that the clippings don't shoot into the neighbor's yard. It was a lot of time spent around my dad doing little things like that. He usually didn't buy new lawn mowers. He refurbished ones other people had thrown out that were piled beside the road. That taught me to use my know-how to run an efficient, cost-effective operation.

Because of the allowance system where I was forced to do my chores with precision and as a self-starter to earn my pay, I learned about the value of money. I loved saving my money! Well, my mom noticed this, too, and realized she could hold money over my head as a way to get me to pay attention to bad habits like leaving my socks in the living room. When something like this would happen, my mom would say, "Put a dollar in the wooden bowl." Having to pay a fine taught me that there would be consequences, and it hit me where it hurt when I lost precious dollars from my bank.

I loathed to vacuum our house growing up. In high school, when I had my first job working as a tour guide at a local children's museum, I realized something. We would have to vacuum the play area in the museum, but I started to see that when I was doing it there I was more motivated than when vacuuming in my own home. Why was that? Perhaps part of it was that I was doing it for a more meaningful reason: I was earning money at the museum. Perhaps part of it was that I was doing it for someone else, and so it meant more to me. It is those times when you don't have the motivation that it's going to help someone else or the motivation that you'll get paid for it that you must remind yourself, "I am doing this for someone. I'm doing this for God. I'm doing it for me." That's when that money test sheds light on my true purpose.

During my time in graduate school in China, I noticed a culture where everyone was very hardworking. Many Chinese people went to work early in the morning and stayed late at night, and that was just a normal thing for them. It was a common sight to walk past a school and see a lot of grandparents there to pick up the children because their parents simply were not available; they were working. Even the Chinese students in my class were much busier than the rest of us. They would take on extra projects working with a professor, having gotten little to no sleep the night before because they were working such long hours. What we think is hard work is relative to our culture, so that we do have to find a balance there. In the case of work and many other aspects of life, deep lessons come when kids and adults are exposed to the ways of other people. These occasions foster introspection that bolsters maturity.

Assignments

1. Answer and discuss with a partner or class the questions below.
2. Recite Luke 4:1–14 from memory. Invite someone to discuss this passage and all its drama with you. Encourage this person to join you in memorizing it.

Chapter 6 Discussion Questions

1. What are some of the possible consequences of failure to develop a serious work ethic in our children? How, if left uncorrected, can children's efforts to squirm out of work evolve into real problems as they grow older? In what ways are the spiritual aspects of this failure more serious?
2. Discuss the longtime advantages of beginning a committed approach to work at an early age. Think of the benefits this kind of perspective has for your children and to perhaps up your own work ethic a few notches. What is it worth to build this kind of character in our children?
3. Allowance or not? What is your practice on giving an allowance? Do you exact penalties for work not done or of poor quality? Consider Claire's reaction to the allowance system. What did she learn? Do you consider this an effective method of teaching an admirable work ethic?
4. Let your kids see you doing work. Haley reinforces this tip in her section of this chapter. What do you consider to be your duty as a parent to equip your child and teach an admirable work ethic that will endure a lifetime? What kind of example are you? Be honest in your self-examination; do some self-policing.
5. Make it manageable. Set a deadline. Rosalind agrees with this strategy. She outlines a procedure of organization for projects that would otherwise be overwhelming. How involved are you in your children's assignments? Do you show them how

to follow through to completion? Give examples of how the proper organization of a lesson is a great way to build a strong work ethic to allow satisfaction for a task well done. What other suggestions do you have?

For Personal Use

Write down the most important concept you gained from chapter 6 in regard to developing spiritual fortitude in kids. You will be asked to do this for each chapter. Then personally review your answers at the conclusion of this twelve-lesson study. What did you learn about yourself? What can you pass on to the next generation(s)?

7

TIME LINE: EXTRA INNINGS

Colleen

In the 1959 film *North by Northwest*, there's a shooting scene in the cafeteria at Mt. Rushmore. The Eva Marie Saint character pulls out a gun and threatens the Cary Grant character. There are a bunch of extras sitting, eating, and talking in the background, seemingly unaware of the dire circumstances unfolding as they enjoy their lunch. Apparently, no one on director Alfred Hitchcock's production team noticed the actions of one of the extras—a little boy. He's wincing, with his ears covered, in anticipation of the coming gunshot.

Some poor continuity person probably got into hot water over that production blunder, but we can enjoy a lesson from it: give your kids inside information so that they can cover their ears and wince before everybody else, before the gunshot. That little boy was able to see the future because he had probably been through the scene several times. We and our children have to march into the future the hard way, but God gives us the prescience to be pretty sure of what is going to happen so that our fortitude rises with uncertainty and our courage with perceived danger.

Are We There Yet?

We don't know how long our lives will last or when Jesus will come back, but we must plan our time line for extra innings, if necessary.

That means we have to conduct ourselves now in such a way as to make provision for long-term goals. In the kingdom of God, the ability to see the future is the skill on which all other abilities rest. There is little success without it. God sees perfectly and with experience what we don't yet see. Fortunately, the Bible schools us in heavenly realities, human nature, and cause and effect so that we can have a reasonably good idea of what's coming next. This chapter's purpose is twofold: (1) help adults strengthen their ability to see and plan far into the future and (2) help adults rear their children to be experts at seeing and planning far into the future.

Kids have little vision; adults need to have vision for them. Adults may have more vision, but if they're like me, it waxes and wanes. We've got to fortify that foresight and set it in concrete to guide our lives so that every step is toward that abiding goal of being a true disciple of Christ and spending eternity with God.

The perspective on time varies from person to person. Some people focus on the past, some on the present, and some on the future. Generally speaking, those who focus on the future, with moderation, of course, are those who plan ahead and act today in ways that will bring those plans to fruition in the decades ahead. This can involve enduring hardship or deprivation now to enjoy success perhaps years or a lifetime away. Having vision for ourselves takes a hard day's work. Having vision on top of that for our kids is exhausting. That's why most people abandon it, if they ever had it.

Seeing the Future

Humans have been fascinated with this idea of knowing the future throughout the annals of history, from Noah and the first weather forecast in Genesis to the present, when some of our most memorable fiction follows this theme (e.g., *It's a Wonderful Life*). From infancy, a prime difference between the immature and the mature is the ability to be fairly sure about what the future holds. A newborn panics and cries like his life depends on it each time he is hungry, because he hasn't learned, like the five-year-old, that food will come soon; no need to despair. As we develop, there comes adroitness in this navigation of life as it unfolds. We fumble, though, when the future throws a risk that brings doubt. That scares us in our limited sight. How we see in the face of crisis or peril is basic in whether or not we will operate as Christians of fortitude, of resolve.

The New Testament is replete with God's injunctions not to fear and substantial—but not yet revealed—justification for remaining brave. God hadn't stated anything new for four hundred years when He chose His first words to be "Do not be afraid" (Luke 1:13), as Gabriel bids Zacharias peace. The angel then promises joy and gladness as the logic behind ceasing to fear. Jesus, on multiple occasions, commands the same conversion from fear to a new emotion or new action with the promise of reward. His listeners will receive the reward if they can only see His future. This capacity to see the future is foundational and complementary to staying power. It propels its possessors headlong and confidently into an unknown and suspect space.

Grit or Not?

Two pertinent biblical examples demonstrate the contrast of grit in action and grit aborted. The differences rest on the ability to envision and believe what is promised ahead so much that threats of pain and death stumble, impotent in the face of faith.

The martyr Stephen punctuates the end of his life by seeing with his eyes the vision that was just as truly in his mind. In his Acts 7 address to the Sanhedrin Council, he must have been feeling the answer to the apostles' earlier prayer asking for boldness in preaching, because this is a bold speech. Stephen begins with the CliffsNotes version of the Old Testament that accelerates to accusations of the betrayal and murder of Jesus and a comparison to the "uncircumcised." It takes pluck to make that jump and assert something so provocative, knowing that other believers had been arrested and beaten by this same council for merely preaching in the name of Jesus.

The respected council members are not about to take this lying down, so they grind their teeth at Stephen in fury. Spiritual toughness emboldens him to look not for a place to hide—but up. Where else would a faithful person look? What he sees prompts him to invite the council member attackers to look up and see "the Son of Man standing at the right hand of God" (Acts 7:56). Stephen sees his future in Jesus standing beside God, and this carries him through the stoning with the courage to ask God to forgive his killers. This is grit in action.

On the other hand, the Old Testament prophet Elijah is an example of grit aborted under duress. Elijah is at first courageous in his challenge to a competition with the prophets of Baal on Mount Carmel (see 1 Kings 18:21). He exhibits unfailing nerve as he honors God and believes fully in His power to defeat the Baal prophets in their own idolatry. God doesn't disappoint as He routs the opponents in this contest, and Elijah executes the false prophets (1 Kings 18:38–40).

However, Elijah's fortitude inexplicably wilts against Jezebel's vengeful death threat, and he hides in a cave. When God asks Elijah what he is doing there, his answer seems to be supplying information, as though God is in the dark on the situational awareness: "I have been very zealous for the Lord God of hosts; for the children of Israel have forsaken Your covenant, torn down Your altars, and killed Your prophets with the sword. I alone am left; and they seek to take my life" (1 Kings 19:10). Elijah's understanding is frail and narrow compared to God's past, present, and future omniscience.

How does Elijah lose his nerve? It appears that Jezebel's personal threats loom large (1 Kings 19:2–3). He is alone (19:4). He is tired and brooding (19:4). Any of these might take the confidence out of his heart, but none will as long as he keeps his vision. The proof is in Elijah's reaction to God's answer to the "I alone am left" comment. With a defeated outlook, Elijah listens as God delivers the surprising news: "Yet I have reserved seven thousand in Israel, all whose knees have not bowed to Baal, and every mouth that has not kissed him" (19:18). Not ten, not one hundred—but seven thousand still digging in along with Elijah. This is the turning point, because Elijah gets to work now with the guts to condemn two kings and perform other works in the service of God. God has filled in the details, revealing that Elijah is not alone—by a long shot—and there is still faith in Israel.

This news refreshes his vision and restores his resolve. If only Elijah had used his ability to see God's everlasting care without a special revelation, he never would have given up.

Time Line: Fifty-Two

Counting on God's words about the future and living by them is fraught with difficulty for His people. If we could be better at it, there would be more faith and less fear. A greater number of momentous things would be accomplished for God's glory—and faster. To see this, let's return to Nehemiah and his comrades a while before they rebuild the Jerusalem walls. In Nehemiah 1:3 Nehemiah hears the bad news about his relatives in Jerusalem: "The survivors who are left from the captivity in the province are there in great distress and reproach. The wall of Jerusalem is also broken down, and its gates are burned with fire." Austin Ziehlke, in his manuscript with the working title of "52 Days to Life" about the book of Nehemiah, points out that "living in a destroyed city broke the spirit of the Jews, and they never realized, in all that time, that they were only 52 days away from having their wall rebuilt. Only 52 days. If they had any idea that it was only going to take 52 days, they most assuredly would have jumped at the prospect of protecting their Temple, families, and way of life" (Ziehlke 2019). This brings up another angle to perspective of time. Look with optimism.

We may cast our eyes far into the future, but if that prospect is gray and gloomy, with overwhelming work before us, we'll have a difficult time sweating for what we see in the abstract ahead. When the Jews in the destroyed Jerusalem looked at the work before them, they may have calculated insurmountable odds and a very long timeline for completion. In reality the final walk-through was less than two months away.

One trick in succeeding is to have a cheerful, smiling outlook, even if we don't feel it at first. We must exhibit this for those we're leading. There will be work, sacrifice, and possibly pain, but if we train our minds to dwell on the joyful finish line instead of the blisters on our feet, it will be easier to continue on course. And who knows, maybe the fruits of our labor will arrive far sooner than we expected, as with Nehemiah's crew.

Haley

Goals are unreachable without telos thinking—thinking about the ultimate aim. If we have the goal in mind, the actions necessary to reach it often follow. I think that's why God gave us a taste of our goal. We read glorious details in the Bible about what heaven will be, and won't it be wonderful there? Sadly, not everyone who claims the heavenly goal spends much time contemplating what it will be like and the work it will take to get there. Without the goal in mind, it's difficult for the actions and thoughts to follow.

God gives us the vision, but the hard part is keeping it always in mind. It's challenging, because we are physical beings as well as spiritual. The immediate, physical part can easily cloud our long perspective of time. If you truly desire and have a clear picture of heaven, it's that much easier to envision yourself doing what keeps you on the straight and narrow path. Give that gift to your children. Teach them to have a vision of the kingdom and to think about it often. With proper training, your children can learn to focus their eyes on the future.

Being in a finance field, I like to think of it in terms of what we know about how people save their money. When you graduated from high school, you probably didn't start saving for retirement right away. That's because you envisioned yourself as your eighteen-year-old self at age eighty. If you're the same at eighty as you are at eighteen, you don't need much—ramen noodles and a couch to sleep on will suffice.

After working for a while, you discovered you had accumulated some money to buy nice things, but you didn't want to be tied to work for the rest of your life. That's when you saw yourself enjoying nice things at eighty and needing money to do that, so the saving began. However, most Americans forget to envision themselves in poor health until they notice their health declining. At fifty, their saving dramatically increases, because to live comfortably in retirement while paying health bills costs serious money. Now, if you'd seen that end point when you graduated from high school (or earlier), your saving would have begun in earnest then, which would make easier the saving in years to come.

It's the same with our souls. If we envision ourselves at the end of life's journey as physical beings, it doesn't make much sense to lay up treasure in heaven. However, as Christians, if we use telos thinking, we think often about the ultimate aim, which is a spiritual one. We save for a greater retirement that is far different from a physical one, and by doing that we are prepared to be welcomed into heaven.

It's not natural to think with the ultimate goal in mind, especially when the physical world is so attractive. That allure tempts us to forget the end as we see what the enticing present offers us. So when you teach your kids to be members of the kingdom of heaven, teach them to think about the future. Here are some ways to do that:

1. Make sure they know what heaven will be like, so they can see the wonderful goal.
2. Practice thinking about heaven often with them.
3. Start when they're young, so it's easier for them to make deposits to their treasure in heaven throughout their lives.

Think of it as the soul's IRA—Imagine Rapture Again.

Rosalind

Uncertainty about the future can be unsettling, but having vision to anticipate a wonderful, spiritual plan unfolding should motivate us to push forward, even into the unknown. Just as when Gabriel appears to Zacharias, Gabriel provides the same reassurance, "Do not be afraid," to Mary when he appears to her to announce that she will be the mother of Jesus. She is startled by his greeting, and she must be even more frightened when she hears his message. She is to be the earthly, virgin mother of the Son of God, who would reign in a never-ending kingdom and bring salvation to the whole world. What a shocking prophecy to hear at such a young age! Gabriel knows she has no reason to fear, and because she has foresight and trusts in the faithfulness of God, she responds by saying, "Let it be to me according to your word," and steps confidently into her future (Luke 1:26–38).

It is a worthy exercise to think back to things I disliked as a kid and realize how much my attitude has changed since then because of vision. Broccoli eating used to be a real chore. I ate it because I was told to, not because I could predict any type of payback in my life or see my future, with or without broccoli. My parents, however, knew the health benefits associated with a life of clean eating and the effect it has on the body over time. Now, as an adult, I eat broccoli because I have acquired a taste for it and because I have adopted the healthful disposition instilled in me so long ago.

In my career I have the opportunity to regularly train new team members. No matter what the training is, one thing I try to highlight is the big picture. How does this particular task fit into the final product? Why is this task important in the long run? Having farsightedness makes the journey more worthwhile.

The same goes for spiritual matters. Memorizing verses, completing Bible lessons, and participating in study sessions are not tasks children naturally gravitate to, and it's difficult for young minds to comprehend deep spiritual thoughts. Adults must emphasize to them often why all of these things are especially important rather than merely force kids to complete assignments. Some added foresight can help children stay on track when they start to get distracted and lose focus on the future.

Claire

Sometimes lessons we learn as children don't feel like lessons until we're grown. Even though we don't have or want a lot of vision as kids, adults know we need those lessons and give them to us anyway. One lesson tied to vision is that of gratitude, or thankfulness.

Thankfulness may seem a bit out of place in a discussion of vision and assets. However, it goes a long way in training young ones to be realistic about the source of blessings and how they will play out in the future. We learned to send thank you notes as children. There's more to it than just saying, "Thanks." People love a personal message about specific appreciation for the giver's generosity or how the gift is being used. This reminded me to be thankful myself as much as it was a way to show my gratitude to someone else. It made us be more aware of what others were doing for us. Writing notes such as this is something we all know is a good thing, but sometimes we forget. However, Jesus believed very much in thankfulness. Surely each of the ten lepers that Jesus healed was delighted, but only one followed through on that feeling and came back to show gratitude, and Jesus noticed (see Luke 17).

Writing thank you notes has become second nature with practice and the reinforcement of seeing the benefits of it over the years. But my current struggle is to remember to thank God. I daily remember to ask God for specific blessings, but I don't daily remember to thank Him for those moments he got me through, for taking my burden away, or for allowing the recovery of a friend. It's more difficult to remember to be grateful to God when we don't see His face or immediate reaction. This has long been man's downfall, to lack gratefulness "because, although they knew God, they did not glorify Him as God, nor were thankful, but became futile in their thoughts, and their foolish hearts were darkened" (Romans 1:21).

I recently received an email from myself that I sent a year ago. It was through futureme.org where you can send an email to your future self. It was eye-opening to see what concerned me a year before. I realized that almost all the things that were consuming my mind back then have floated away. At the time some of the things seemed like they would never pass. God was with me throughout those times. But how could it be that I forgot to thank him? This is where I believe reflection can be a good practice, to think where I was a day, week, month, or year ago.

Assignments

1. Answer and discuss with a partner or class the questions below.
2. Grab a partner and have him or her follow along in the Bible to check accuracy as you recite Luke 4:1–14 from memory.

Chapter 7 Discussion Questions

1. This chapter's purpose is twofold: (1) help adults strengthen their ability to see and plan far into the future and (2) help adults rear their children to be experts at seeing and planning far into the future. What procedures or steps do you see as necessary in laying a course of action to reach these goals? At what age do you think this plan should begin for your children? Discuss how tenacity is necessary in this long-term process.
2. Talk about some Bible examples of those who faced various crises, perils, and doubts but still endured until the end. Consider the passage in Hebrews chapter 11 (especially v. 13–16). What qualities of character do these examples portray? Would you say that our lives today are easier or harder than theirs? Does this make any difference in our need for perseverance?
3. With reference to Haley's section, in what way do you describe heaven to your children? As you help the younger ones with their lessons, do you apply each current story to the ultimate goal of heaven? Some of the stories may be about punishment—how do you relate those with regard to eternity? Haley points out that we are competing today with an attractive physical world—we must teach our kids to think about the future. How do you plan to do this?
4. With reference to Rosalind's section, how can you help your child to overcome fear of the future? (Refer to Hebrews 13:6.) What can you do to train him or her to build a lifelong trust

in God? List specific ways you help him or her to see the big picture and the end result of a life of learning about God and of service to Him. Comment on this statement: the more we learn of God through His word, the more our anticipation of heaven is enhanced.

5. With reference to Claire's section, Christians should be the most thankful persons on earth. In view of what God has done for us, we should be evermore grateful to Him. Cite Bible passages regarding our need to give thanks to God. Do our prayers contain more requests of what we want God to do for us and less of thanksgiving to Him? What effect does an attitude of ingratitude have on one's character? Do you see future problems from this—both spiritually and socially? To emulate God, what should be our behavior toward others? Describe and give specific examples.

For Personal Use

Write down the most important concept you gained from chapter 7 in regard to developing spiritual courage in kids. You will be asked to do this for each chapter. Then personally review your answers at the conclusion of this twelve-lesson study. What did you learn about yourself? What can you pass on to the next generation? Hopefully, this will have been a profitable study for you.

8

SCREENING THE SCREEN

Colleen

I have a career's worth of experience with screens. More specifically, my expertise lies in producing content that keeps viewers looking at the screen instead of looking at something else. In my work as a game developer, my team has produced serious games where the content is not just for fun but for learning. So I know how it works.

The screen, with its digital magic, is a useful tool for all of us. However, it can reach the point of diminishing returns when it holds us spellbound. It may trump the message of the Bible or interactions with family and friends. The pleasure and ease of its entertainment can encroach on our legitimate pursuits. What activities and relationships are we trading for another round of a computer game? Could the screen and its communication take the place of the physical world and the human beings around us?

It's not a fair fight, especially when children's young minds are on the line. The professionals programming media content are trained in ways to attract users' attention, even to addict. Their jobs may depend on it. Their careers are built on it. Kids aren't self-disciplined enough to regulate consumption. If the programming is pleasing, they will consume. It is up to the adults to judiciously monitor these activities. We must screen the screen.

Doing your own research on this topic is fairly easy. We already have documented cases where parents are no match for the dopamine addiction their children develop toward computer games. I could write a whole book about it, but for now, let's start with this one chapter.

Olden-Day Screens versus Twenty-First Century Screens

Kids have always been looking for a buzz, but for previous generations the buzz had a natural end. For instance, swinging, fast rides, and sports eventually exhaust us or run out of gasoline. Even when radio and TV came along, the content was expensive to produce and therefore not plentiful enough to run twenty-four hours a day. Most of it was not that interesting to kids, except for Saturday morning cartoons. While my parents did consciously restrict our time in front of the TV, even if they hadn't, back then most programming couldn't hold a candle to playing sports, climbing trees, and riding bikes.

In the twenty-first century, sophisticated animation and special effects have greatly improved the experience for television and film viewers. Add to that the interactive nature of video games, where the player has control, and today's content is very difficult to beat. Throw in neuroscientists' engineering and 24/7 access, and you have an endless dopamine trigger that can be tailored to the individual child to addict more efficiently. Parents buy this trigger from a legitimate business for the child's birthday. It seems innocuous, and the child lights up when he or she opens that present. It's very gratifying for parents and loved ones to see this. The World Health Organization has added "gaming disorder" to its list of diseases.

I know a Christian couple whose son was a game addict as early as fifth grade, according to his mother. Along with the game playing came bad behavior, such as habitual lying about any subject. The punishments for disobeying his parents' mandates to resist the games were swift, strict, and involved loss of all privileges, but he was willing to lose his rights and his dignity for a few minutes of game play.

The boy's parents learned more than once that the only way he could resist another round was to be locked out of all devices at home and at school and then be constantly supervised. If his parents let up in any way on their supervision of him, their son was right back in the thick of his game habit. Once they found him in his closet in the middle of the night playing a forbidden game.

In addition, although the parents have restricted their son's game playing, his peers are still freely absorbed in it. Even in spiritually related settings, this presents further issues since their son's interaction with his friends and peers inevitably brings conversations and activities related to gaming. His mother laments, "That's all his friends talk about. We tell him that the purpose to visiting with friends after [church] services is to talk to them, not huddle around a screen." Clearly, countering the game and entertainment lure requires daily strategy refining and adjustment.

Age-Old Fight

The battle for children's minds has been around since ancient times, so we have the advantage of biblical example. In Nehemiah 13:23–25, the prophet experiences a disturbing revelation:

> In those days I also saw Jews who had married women of Ashdod, Ammon, and Moab. And half of their children spoke the language of Ashdod, and could not speak the language of Judah, but spoke according to the language of one or the other people. So I contended with them and cursed them, struck some of them and pulled out their hair, and made them swear by God, saying, "You shall not give your daughters as wives to their sons, nor take their daughters for your sons or yourselves."

Nehemiah's reaction is extreme; obviously the Jews had not protected the next generation from the ways of other cultures. Are we capable of such an extreme reaction? Could we even answer objectively when asked if we have allowed the twenty-first century version of this to happen? Do our kids know all the movie soundtrack lyrics and sports team stats but can't be bothered to memorize scripture? Is the world etched on their hearts? Do they speak the language of the world instead of the communication of God's word and the lyrics of praise hymns? We all must live in the world, but "friendship with the world is enmity with God" (James 4:4). What is your status?

Jesus and faithful people in the Bible enjoy good meals, financial aid, wedding celebrations, and travel upon boats and fast animals, so we know that pleasure is a blessing from God. However, our pursuit of gratification can become skewed so that it crowds out our true purpose on this earth—to love God above all else and to love our neighbor as ourselves.

The Value of Time

To help ourselves and our kids develop the kind of strong minds that can navigate the pleasures of entertainment and technology without giving them our best years, a principal consideration is time and ways of seeing it. Using time wisely drives many inner forces that bring strength, like willpower and self-discipline. We must condition ourselves to see time as a commodity needed to accomplish things and a treasure to be guarded greedily.

Computer games, movies, social media, and the like steal our time. Media content lures us into the world of happy endings. However, siblings need to interact and squabble so that they understand how to solve problems with people. Children need to learn to sit next to a sweaty, wiggly little sister in order to become tolerant and know how to divert their attention to things other than the annoyance in the back seat. Children must learn how to navigate the unfairness of the real world. If I had it to do over again, I would devote even more planning and conscientiousness to teaching my children from a young age the precious nature of time and how to manage it.

Personally, I have seen how this mindset brings to the battle a tenacity for controlling my own time instead of giving it away to low-value activities. Other people and factors try to wrench away my time from me and my service to God. Given another go-round, I would teach my kids to be even more shrewd in matters of time. Ephesians 5:15–17 urges, "See then that you walk circumspectly, not as fools but as wise, redeeming the time, because the days are evil. Therefore do not be unwise, but understand what the will of the Lord is." Jesus had another forty days to spend with the human race after His resurrection. What did He do in His last forty days? He appeared to hundreds of people, and He taught. He redeemed the time.

One important way to "buy back" time for your young ones is to restrict access to the media and digital entertainment that chew up their youth. This may mean parents and other relatives must work on their own self-discipline with these devices. Some parents are also hooked on screens and are tempted to let their kids continue in front of games and entertainment because it keeps peace and leaves the parents to their own pursuits.

My husband, Wally, and I determined to keep the TV, phones, and digital content in a small compartment of our daughters' lives. We gradually scaled back until we did not have cable TV and greatly restricted the kids' access to broadcast programming. They did watch some films. We were especially concerned about all the things they wouldn't be doing if they habitually watched TV and other entertainment. One important result was that our daughters didn't see commercials very often, limiting the temptations they bring. In my short experience, I feel confident that conditioning our children to reach for a ball, musical instrument, book, pen, etc. instead of an ON button preserved their valuable childhood years for more meaningful things.

Don't Fall for These Ploys from Kids

Other parents and I have discussed our experiences in helping our children weigh the validity of potential careers. Sometimes children figure out that their parents will sanction more hours of fun if they can be justified as paving the way to a potential career. Here are a few maneuvers to watch out for.

1. "I need to play more video games because I want to be a game developer when I grow up." Playing computer games for hours a day is not the way to prepare. Send this kid to a serious class on programming, preferably one on 3-D programming for games. This is messy-algebra-equations-on-the-whiteboard, laborious programming. A rigorous class will deliver the reality. Also, have him do research to learn exactly what a career in games involves. Check out job stability and questions of the morality of game content. I knew the parents of a teenager who convinced them that playing more video games would prepare him for a game programming career. All it prepared him for was to sit in his dorm room playing video games and skipping class, eventually flunking out of college.
2. "I can't learn unless I have this game or app." Kids must be good readers and learners so that it takes a minimal amount of effort to teach them new subjects. The cheapest way is for them to learn from text. If they have to have multimedia or games or a teacher to lecture, it costs more money. Developing games and multimedia has an astronomically higher price than printing a textbook. Your child will be much easier to teach, and an asset to the organization, if she can get information on her own from a book.
3. "I need to watch more movies because I want to be a movie director when I grow up." Watching more films is not the answer. If children truly want to go into the film industry, send them over to their grandparents' house with a video camera. Have them produce their first documentary using original interviews. Or have them write an original screenplay, put together a storyboard, and shoot it with actors and homemade scenery. Then send them to a class on editing. All of this will give them a taste of the difficulty of the work and how hard it is to make art come alive on video. Again, do research to find out the competitive nature and long-term opportunities of careers in film.

Fight for Their Souls and Their Childhoods

When I was visiting California, a man told me that he and his wife vacation in a town there where people congregate in shops and restaurants, talking to each other and interacting. You don't see cell phones or other devices to absorb their attention, because the redwoods are so tall and broad that they block cell service. Maybe we should learn from the redwoods. Parents and other adults must stand as the towering trees to preserve their kids' childhoods, to monitor closely what they are encountering on the internet. We must limit screen preoccupation and move them back to real life. We redwoods are bigger. We are older and more experienced. We know what is good for kids to help them develop relationships and teamwork with other people, including those of all ages, not just kids. We know how to feed them God's word to nourish their souls and prepare them for a life of belonging to God and glorifying Him.

My friend Ray told me of a scene he witnessed while looking out his office window at a children's playground below. A little girl was sitting inside a toy car, playing, enjoying herself. A little boy walked over and stood a few feet away. Then he inched closer to the car. The girl kept playing. The boy inched even closer. This went on until the boy stood right next to the car. After a while the boy opened the car door and just stood there for a while. Then he slowly climbed into the car. The girl got out of the car and walked away. Ray said this was a good analogy for the way things often work in this world. This feels more and more correct as I have pondered this episode in the decades since.

The little girl obviously prized the car. However, without a word the boy gently hijacked it from her. She put up no fight—she gave it to him without even an argument. I'm afraid to say that I am watching parents hand over their boys' and girls' lives to movie directors and game developers in a similar sad scene. This simply will not do if our young ones have any hope of flourishing as normal adults and faithful, on-duty Christians who know how to interact and care about people; who know how to withstand disappointment and the struggles of life; and who can move into the world of others to spread the gospel.

At a game developers conference, I listened to a keynote speaker lay out the dilemma he and his programmers strategize over. Should they make the game challenging so that players fail if they choose the wrong path? Or should they program the game so that the players usually win, so that they are happy and keep coming back as customers? He knew the better experience is to allow realistic consequences. He also knew players don't want the pain of losing; they want the euphoria of victory. Digital games can always deliver a positive outcome. The real world delivers a few wins and many, many hard knocks that polish us into shining stones. What will your children get? What they want or what's best for them?

Haley

One of the most powerful tools Satan has to make us soft and apathetic is inactivity, and he's wielding it more skillfully than ever. He has disguised doing nothing as relaxation, recreation, education, and an ever-present and necessary part of our lives. For the most part, the king of lies still reigns when he convinces us to believe that spending time with screens is all these things. Truthfully, a large portion of our time with screens is distracting from what needs to be done and wasteful of the valuable time we've been given. It engenders inactivity, which is perhaps the easiest way Satan can keep us from our Christian work.

In Luke 10:38–42 Jesus chides Martha for being distracted away from spiritual enterprises. When she urges Him to send Mary into the kitchen instead of allowing her to sit at His feet and absorb His word, He says, "Martha, Martha, you are worried and troubled about many things. But one thing is needed, and Mary has chosen that good part, which will not be taken away from her" (v. 41–42). Note that Martha isn't absorbed in some fun game; she is doing a lot of serving others and needs help. Even in this case, Jesus makes the severe point that of the two choices, Mary's is more valuable and lasting.

Screens, entertainment, and social media can quickly become distractions. I see many parents who apparently don't understand it that way, though. Instead they might say something like this: "What I show my kids through screens is teaching them great information, and it keeps them occupied so I can do important work. How is there a downside to that?" What I see in addition to this is kids who learn to rely on screens to stay occupied and parents who are replaced by content programmers who want nothing more than to make money.

I grew up in a time when people watched TV more than ever. Someone I know said, "When I think about it, I was raised by the TV. When I wasn't in school, I was watching TV, and nobody monitored what I watched." That person had access to relatively little content compared to what kids have today. It's a scary thought that some elementary-school-age kids of Christians I know have their own cell phones and almost unlimited access to the internet. The parents aren't in control of what goes into their kids' minds, and God's word certainly doesn't guide what the internet has in store for them.

Even if the content kids are seeing through screens is wholesome, screens can be of danger to Christians. When I started college, I went to church at a congregation with a large group of college students. It was great to be around people my age who had good intentions, but their devices had gotten in the way of their spiritual focus. One of the elders of that congregation met with us and told us about the problem. He said that from the vantage point of the audio booth, which was above the section where the college students sat together, anyone could see that many students were on their cell phones during worship. And it was determined that they weren't using the phones to read their Bibles. Though it may be easy to rear kids with the help of screens, it is more important than ever to teach them not to rely on them. If kids aren't controlled by screens, that's one less way Satan can tempt them.

Rosalind

The American Psychiatric Association published a list of nine symptoms that point toward a diagnosis of internet gaming disorder (Petry, et al. 2014). Looking through the list, I noticed that there are several symptoms that bring to mind Bible verses. A disorder or addiction may take a physical or mental toll on the sufferer; focusing on the following verses could be useful when dealing with such issues:

- Symptom: Withdrawal symptoms when gaming is taken away or not possible (sadness, anxiety, irritability).
  God's Wisdom: "Be anxious for nothing, but in everything by prayer and supplication, with thanksgiving, let your requests be made known to God" (Philippians 4:6).
- Symptom: Deceiving family members or others about the amount of time spent on gaming.
  God's Wisdom: "For from within, out of the heart of men, proceed evil thoughts, adulteries, fornications, murders, thefts, covetousness, wickedness, deceit, lewdness, an evil eye, blasphemy, pride, foolishness" (Mark 7:21–22).
- Symptom: Continuing to game despite problems.
  God's Wisdom: "If your right eye causes you to sin, pluck it out and cast it from you; for it is more profitable for you that one of your members perish, than for your whole body to be cast into hell" (Matthew 5:29).
- Symptom: Preoccupation with gaming.
  God's Wisdom: "Set your mind on things above, not on things on the earth" (Colossians 3:2).
- Symptom: The use of gaming to relieve adverse moods, such as guilt or helplessness.
  God's Wisdom: "Now may the God of hope fill you with all joy and peace in believing, that you may abound in hope by the power of the Holy Spirit" (Romans 15:13).

All gaming, social media, and general screen time is not necessarily bad. There are actually thought to be some potential benefits, such as educational profits, social interaction, and the improvement of motor skills. If you decide to allow some screen time in your home, try focusing on managing the time wisely. I knew a dad who chose to let his kids have cell phones, but every evening he and his wife collected the devices before bedtime.

If you live in a home with two parents, be sure both are on board with the rules. This eliminates one parent being the "mean parent" and emphasizes to the kids that the parents are a team and the rules apply to everyone in the home. Kids love to approach parents separately to push boundaries.

What about treating gaming time as a reward only, not a standard, everyday event? For instance, if all chores are completed at the end of the week, a certain amount of gaming is allowed, but only as an allowance of sorts. Or every minute spent playing a game requires the same amount of time to be put toward preparing a meal for someone in need, playing outside, helping a sibling, practicing an instrument, or reading the Bible.

If you don't yet have children or they are not old enough to be affected by a gaming preoccupation, consider this: Don't start. If you never allow screen time to get out of control, there is no need to come back around and try to fix the problem. If you are trying to fix the problem, hang in there and do not give up.

Claire

Video games instill a false sense of security to try until you succeed. There are unlimited chances after failing in video games. However, in real life we don't always have a second chance. For example, there's no replay for the soccer game you just lost, no redo if a girl rejects your offer to go on a date; you don't get to retake the test you failed, and there's no do-over on the job interview you bombed. Children need to learn that there's not always a second chance and also how to accept and move on from a failure.

Children can learn these lessons if they are engaged in meaningful activities that provide the risk of disappointment, as in real life. Parents can create activities in which there is a competitive spirit. For example, play a game to see which child can answer the most Bible trivia questions correctly or which child can memorize the most Bible verses. Taking this step requires that parents be creative with providing real-world games and activities. At the same time, there must be limits on access to computer games, the same way parents make restrictions on junk food and spending money.

Imagine handing off your car keys to a five-year-old. He or she would love to drive; it'd be fun. But would you do it? No! That child simply isn't old enough to handle all that goes along with maneuvering a big machine. Apply this logic to kids' access to computer games, and be honest when you calculate how many hours your children spend interacting with screens each day.

A friend of mine, Milton, likes to tell the story of something that occurred when he was a young boy that was pivotal in shaping his use of video games and media. He and his brother could play video games only after their father arrived home from work. This was not because they were such disciplined children but because only their father knew how to set up the game console to the TV. It was not until they were older that they realized that setting up the console merely entailed the simple task of plugging in a couple of audiovisual cords.

This was their dad's way of limiting playtime to just when he could monitor it. In a more modern example, iPads can be set with a password. It is important for parents to act as gatekeepers through these controls in order to limit their children's time on devices. Just like the car keys and the audiovisual cords, we shouldn't give our children the "keys" to something they don't have the forethought and wisdom to use with restraint.

Assignments

1. Take a measure of how much time you spend per week surfing the internet for fun, checking email and social media, and playing computer games. Now tally up the same for your children. Try to be as objective as possible. Consider the number of hours totaled. Does it alarm you? What could you and your kids be doing that would be of more value?
2. Answer and discuss with a partner or class the questions below.

Chapter 8 Discussion Questions

1. What is your reaction to the subject matter of this chapter? Are you aware of the addictive possibilities of TV, social media, and video games for your child—or even yourself? How many hours per day are your kids spending with screens? Add to this time spent at school, work, sports, travel time, eating, sleeping, etc. How much time is left for God?
2. How valuable is time? Computer games, movies, social media, etc. steal our time. This is in direct opposition to the admonition that we redeem the time (Ephesians 5:15–17). What do you do to reinforce this command? Do you prioritize worship time, Bible study, and other spiritual matters, or do you allow for the "I didn't have time" excuse? List some ways you teach your kids to be good stewards of their time. How do you show your kids the dangers of wasting the time we've been given?
3. Because of the interactive nature of many video games, the player has control. The popularity of and excessive participation in these games has led the American Psychiatric Association toward an official diagnosis of "internet gaming disorder." Discuss the symptoms mentioned by Rosalind. What other health hazards are possible (e.g., eye damage, back/ spinal problems, lack of exercise, excessive competitive/

aggressive behavior toward others)? This leads to the question, who or what has the real control?

4. Remember that the objective of this course of study is grit—rearing children to be spiritually strong, persevering, and strategic to develop willpower and self-discipline. We are not talking about a game but about the real world and how children can learn to navigate through its unfairness. What can you do to prepare them to withstand the disappointments and to endure the struggles of life? List some ways you help your children develop relationships and teamwork with other people. What is the importance of teaching them to interact with and care about people of all ages? Are you equipping them to be able to carry God's word into the world?
5. Cell phones—who doesn't have one? Elementary school kids to one-hundred-year-olds talk, text, and take selfies. Cell phones have invaded our lives, even our churches. What control do you have over your child's use of the phone? What rules have you established for its use? How do you handle infringements to the rules?
6. What restrictions have you set on your children's access to computer games and social media? Discuss any resistance to these rules. How did you handle this? What penalties have you had to impose? What danger signals have you taught your children to watch for with regard to predators who infiltrate gaming and social media sites?

For Personal Use

Write down the most important concept you gained from chapter 8 in regard to developing spiritual persistence in kids. You will be asked to do this for each chapter. Then personally review your answers at the conclusion of this twelve-lesson study. What did you learn about yourself? What can you pass on to the next generation? Hopefully, this will have been a profitable study for you.

9

BIBLE CLASS TEACHERS: OVERLOOKED ALLIES

Colleen

To see a child's face reflect the gratification of knowing the right answer or comprehending a new biblical principle—that's the prize moment for Bible class teachers. There was a boy in my class one time who usually couldn't give me a correct answer. He also wasn't reciting his memory verse. I figured he didn't pay attention in class or was a little delayed developmentally. I let his family member know that he needed help memorizing at home. I was puzzled by the lack of enthusiasm to supply that help. However, the next class period, the boy was ready to say his verse of scripture. He recited it perfectly; he just beamed.

It was perhaps a year later that I found out about this student's severe learning disability that prevented him from retaining information, and I remembered the incident with the memory verse. His family member probably had seen my request for him to learn the verse as nearly impossible. However, someone must have worked with him and proved that he could remember, albeit with intense tutoring. Just as important was that rare and overwhelming feeling of accomplishment this boy experienced. I wish his family members had witnessed it. Parents miss a lot, and they don't realize it. I know I didn't fully get it when I dropped off my little girls at the Bible classroom door.

I have taught children's Bible class at four congregations over approximately thirty-four years. If I averaged four students per year, that comes to 136 students total. Just an estimate. My experience covers my single adult years as a brand new Christian, the years married with babies and small children, and on through to the present. Four discoveries have materialized:

1. Bible class teachers are quite accomplished and mostly unseen in action by other Christians.
2. Bible class teachers and parents can be a formidable blitz against Satan, sin, and the world.
3. Parents would be surprised at the joys and adversities they miss in that petri dish of biblical education.
4. Bible class is profitable like no other activity in a child's spiritual training.

Bible Class Teachers Are Quite Accomplished and Mostly Unseen

Many of the remarkable Bible scholars I have known were teaching your kids and mine in Bible class. This occurred to me a few years ago, and I have only wanted to tell more people and with more zeal since. Jesus says, "A disciple is not above his teacher, but everyone who is perfectly trained will be like his teacher" (Luke 6:40). Our children will enjoy a significant blessing if they are like the teachers I've seen. But it's ironic that these scholars have slim audiences—just a handful of students and maybe another teacher. No one else ventures back to the classroom, as far as I know. There's a world of difference between stating by secondhand information that "we have great Bible class teachers" and actually witnessing it.

However, these disciples keep diligently teaching "every creature," with God's word landing on clean little slates that haven't comprehended it before. These teachers can rattle off Bible names, events, and locations without hesitation. They recall on the spot which ones were the good kings and the names of the bad. Like the back of their hand, they know Nebuchadnezzar's dream—the metals, the countries, and where they fit. Paul's journeys? No problem. They can lead a bunch of kids through a question-and-answer overview of the entire Bible lickety-split. All of us should take every opportunity to encourage and work with teachers to make sure our children get the most from this praiseworthy influence.

In my third grade Bible class one time, we were playing a book of Acts board game. A child drew a "Stump the Teacher" card. His mission was to choose a teacher and ask her a question from the book of Acts in an attempt to stump her. One rule was that he had to be able to do whatever he asked of her.

He chose a teacher and asked her to recite the list we had learned of the main point of each chapter of Acts—in reverse order, so starting with chapter 28. He admitted he couldn't do this. I told him his request was rejected because of that, not to mention that the teacher had just rotated into the class and had not been there for the Acts lessons. The teacher overruled me and wanted to try to say the main points of all twenty-eight chapters backward. And she did it impromptu—to the amazement of us all.

Bible class teachers sit in a hot seat few would assume. It's different from preaching, where listeners don't ask questions. Even in an adult Bible class, students are reserved in what they ask the teacher in front of everyone. All bets are off in a kids' class. One time a girl in my third grade Bible class asked if boys marrying boys and girls marrying girls is in the Bible. On the spot I gave the class a short answer, and next class period I offered several Bible verses to help the students learn more.

Teachers also gain great insight about what these young souls are truly thinking because of their natural candor. In Bible class when I was explaining the responsibilities of husbands and wives in marriage, a boy mused, "When I'm the husband, I can tell everybody what to do." I was glad to know his plans so that we could explore them further based on scripture. His future wife may thank me one day.

Bible Class Teachers and Parents Can Be a Formidable Blitz

Teachers are among the people keeping watch over your children's souls. That makes them certain allies. However, my view is that teachers are overlooked partners. Parents need all the firepower they can muster in the battle for their children's eternity. It is with Bible class teachers that mothers and fathers can stand shoulder-to-shoulder against the onslaughts of Satan, sin, and the world. Proverbs 24:6 informs, "For by wise counsel you will wage your own war, And in a multitude of counselors there is safety." I can't think of a parent who wouldn't agree with this—in theory—but in practice abounding opportunities may fall through the cracks. I know exactly what our class lessons will be each year. We talk about obeying your parents, taking care of people, and writing "thank you" notes. I wonder how often the teachers have bolstered a principle over which the parents have been struggling and children are rejecting at home. I'll guess that it happens often; the kids won't let on—that's for sure.

A teacher of an elementary-school-age Bible class told me that she has had one parent—besides those who are fellow teachers—ask how their child is doing in class. I assumed she meant one parent that year. She clarified that she meant one parent in twenty-nine years. She added that she used to ask the kids if they were talking to their parents about their lessons, and they always said "no," so she quit asking. It was depressing to her. Another experienced teacher said that generally no parents ask about the school-age children she teaches. However, when she's in a baby class, there are many questions and concerns from parents.

My experience is similar. There are parents I know well who do approach me to ask how their children are doing in Bible class, but I estimate that the vast majority of the parents of my students over the years did not ask about class at all. I strongly recommend keeping tabs on how things are going for three main benefits: 1. If I know parents support me, I perform better, and the kids profit. 2. If there is a problem, I am more likely to talk to the parents if they have voiced interest in their child's performance. 3. If I have an ongoing familiarity with the parents, I am more likely to mention them in class, to their children's delight. This also reminds students that the teachers and parents are a united force.

One time I gave a review test to my class. Most of the kids bombed it. I marked the incorrect answers, gave them back, and told the students to bring them to the next class corrected. At the next class, I asked one boy if he had his test. He boldly told me, "My dad says you'll have to wait." This was not only disheartening to me, but it also revealed that I had no parental support there. The boy's mother and father were leaders in that congregation. In this exercise there was not much support from most of the other parents either.

On the other hand, I have spoken to parents occasionally about their children's failure to complete assignments or about discipline problems. The parents said the situation would be corrected, and boy, was it. Now, I'm not asking for a group hug, but I can't reinforce enough that teachers and parents are much more effective together than unyoked.

Parents Would Be Surprised at the Joys and Adversities They Missed

I'll start with the adversities. One time a child's parent came to me expressing concern that the other kids in class were making fun of the child. From what I had observed over months in the classroom, if anything it was this child who was gloating about his correct answers and pointing out failures of the other kids. This highlights an inherent complication of operating in a closed learning environment. Unless the parents are also teachers in the room, they may draw a skewed perception of what goes on. It could be skewed toward what a teacher tells the parents or, probably more likely, spun toward the child's way of seeing it.

I have known scores of Bible class teachers, and I can't think of one who was in that role for the glory or any self-expansion. At best they were teaching to fulfill the Great Commission, to glorify God.

At worst they were there because there was a shortage of teachers. I don't recall any teachers being too hard on the students, too exacting. I have seen occasions of letting children take advantage or allowing children to show disrespect.

Teaching periods can be exhilarating, but every now and then they're a real grind. That's when this verse comes to mind: "As iron sharpens iron, So a man sharpens the countenance of his friend" (Proverbs 27:17). Shaping children into sharp people who know God takes wits and creativity, not to mention a lot of nerve. I don't like to change, so I'm one step ahead of students when I suggest that they must change the way they think and conduct themselves according to God's word.

On the one hand, I estimate that about 90 percent of the kids I've taught were very well-behaved and caused no problem whatsoever. On the other hand, I have had young children outright defy me when I told them to move forward one row. I have had a boy kick me under the table. I told him not to let that happen again. He did it again. One time a child stole a key from the room and then lied about it. I have had to tell students to fill out their own homework sheets, as opposed to having their parents do it. In all of these cases, I didn't tell the moms and dads. For the most part, the students and I rectified these problems together. Believe me when I testify that parents would be surprised at the adversities they miss because they aren't witnesses in the classroom.

Another word of counsel: bring your children to class a few minutes early if you want them to enjoy the enrichment activities available and to interact with the other students. In my classroom there are all kinds of activity boards, maps, and artifact displays the kids can experience. I'd like to be able to get to all of these during class time, but after explaining the biblical plot and theme of the lesson, there's not a lot of time for enrichment.

Also, bringing kids to class a little early allows time to recite the memory verse. If they spend a lot of time learning it and then arrive to class leaving no time to say it for the teacher, that's disappointing after all that effort.

Mothers and fathers also miss gratifying and even comical moments as the learning environment unfolds in real time like an improv routine. There was a girl who previously attended Bible class but then returned only occasionally and seemed a little uncomfortable. The rapport with the other kids was not like it had been, simply because of her absence. However, when she did come, there was one girl who ran to meet her and give her a hug with genuine sentiment. All the other kids took this girl's lead and walked over to greet their long-absent friend. It was an important scene for all involved. The parents missed it.

They also missed the time during a game in class when I asked a student, "What helpful young preacher did Paul meet in Lystra?" He answered, "A snake." I was dumbfounded. I had recently noted that the kids didn't seem to be retaining information we were teaching. But this answer was just bizarre. I voiced my bewilderment that our lessons obviously weren't effective if this was the best answer he could recall. Just then he said, "I thought you said 'creature,' like the snake that bit him." We all had a good belly laugh over that one.

Each year it's comical to watch the reactions students exhibit when I first tell them they can memorize a whole chapter of the Bible on their own if they want to. There's no tangible reward, no winner. I explain that as they make progress, they can recite for me in class. Most of the students keep a poker face, but a few let out an emphatic, "Nah!" or an incredulous, "Why would I do that?" By the way, each year some of the students do actually memorize a whole chapter.

Then there was the student who was preoccupied with the worksheet I left lying on the table. On one side the worksheet was blank; on the other side, the answers were filled in. Sometimes the answer side was visible, and he just couldn't get his mind off that. I told him not to worry about it, but he kept bugging me. I told him not to look at the answers, but that didn't quiet him. Finally, one time I had all the students fill in the answers on their own and left the worksheet lying on the table answer side up. The boy quickly filled out his sheet and missed most, if not all, the answers. I had fixed up a fake worksheet completed with wrong answers. I never heard another peep out of him.

Bible Class Is Profitable Like No Other Activity

For a long time, while I fiercely supported church Bible classes, I also thought that their role was as icing on the cake for the kids whose parents are Christians. I felt that if, hypothetically, those children could not come to class anymore, they would still receive a rich and full spiritual upbringing. But as my teaching experience gains breadth, depth, and a more mature angle, I have discovered the vast storehouse of edification that regular Bible class delivers, reinforcing other training but most importantly carrying its own unique supply of spiritual determination. It has value like no other religious discipline.

Bible class is structured and already on the schedule. Rain or shine, it goes on. Someone has invested a great deal of thought and effort in developing lesson plans and materials. The apostle Paul exhorts Timothy, "Preach the word! Be ready in season and out of season. Convince, rebuke, exhort, with all longsuffering and teaching" (2 Timothy 4:2). In this way Bible class is always open for business.

Bible class covers the entire Bible systematically. The kids' classes I have taught generally cover either the Old Testament or New Testament in one year. It's a methodical, chronological treatment of the Bible in an overview. That means various topics come up in discussion that may not commonly emerge in parents' daily interactions with their children. Here are some: betrayal, denial, childbirth, circumcision, humility, faith, stoning. One time I asked a class what "amen" means. When no one knew, I explained the definition and said it is not necessary to end a prayer with the word. One boy seemed relieved and said he thought you would go to hell if you didn't say "amen" at the end of a prayer.

Bible class mixes in other people's perspectives and life experiences. My husband and I seized daily opportunities to teach godliness to our children, which was highly valuable. However, it was just our way of looking at things, mostly our experiences. Bible class brings in a whole new cuisine's worth of tasty morsels to help children see things from someone else's angle. The other students love to tell life experiences as they relate to our lessons, and they share their faith. My childhood stories about someone stealing my bike and kids bullying me give my students a new context for old teachings. Bible class teachers improvise to show kids how to work, how to learn, and ways of seeing life in the kingdom of God. How to respect authority. How to never give up.

Bible class brings a new setting in which kids can succeed. Sometimes parents or other teachers warn me that a child has a learning disability. Over the decades that I have taught, I recall only two cases where the child truly was greatly hindered by a bona fide disability. In most cases I found the problem to be just a lack of self-discipline or failure to practice reading, writing, or paying attention.

We proved this in one case where a child was reading far below grade level. Since reading is essential to getting around in the Bible, the other teachers and I encouraged the girl to read out loud in class with the other children. She did read but would try her best to dodge it. Coincidentally, another teacher was a professional reading tutor. She worked independently with the girl, bringing her up one grade level in a short time, as I recall. There's something about being away from their parents' shield that presses children to mature. They all grow in Bible class.

Haley

You'd be hard-pressed to find a Christian parent who wouldn't agree that Bible class is a laudable tool for raising godly children. However, I have seen a mistake made by even the most well-meaning of parents that negates the benefit of the selfsame tool. This mistake can instantly turn a receptive student into one who feels entitled to direct her own Bible class education rather than learning from an experienced teacher. The mistake is making excuses for one's children.

I was in Bible class as a young girl with several children whose parents made excuses for them. One excuse went something like this:

"My child is extremely smart, and the curriculum in the class is not stimulating. My child doesn't need to do the preparation work for this class." Another went like this: "My child doesn't feel comfortable in Bible class with other kids. My child can come to the adult class with me." As a kid I knew these excuses by parents were the result of the efforts of the children to get out of the hard parts of preparing for class. As an adult and a teacher, I see that these excuses serve only to hurt the children they're made for.

Every time parents make an excuse for their child, the child learns something—he's no dummy. That boy or girl learns that the Bible class teacher has no authority in the classroom. If a parent can nullify anything in the classroom, why would a child have respect for the authority of the teacher? Here's how the thought process goes: 1. My parent told the teacher I don't have to prepare for the next Bible lesson. 2. Doing the Bible lesson must not be important. 3. The other things the teacher tells me to do are not important.

As a result the Bible class becomes unimportant to the child, who decides anything that is difficult or unpleasant in class need not be done. With this conclusion those benefits of having your child taught the Bible by another Christian will not be realized, and you are no longer an ally with the teacher.

Weakening the value of Bible class is but a short-term consequence of teaching children to make excuses. In the longer term, the effects can be more problematic. My job as a college professor puts me near many students who are at the end of their parental raising, and it's very apparent in the ones whose parents made excuses for them. Perennially, I have students who ask for the addition of points to their grade when the semester is done and they don't have the score they would like. They don't ask for points in exchange for additional work to prove they have mastered the material. They ask for points "because I have to graduate this semester." These students expect me to cave to their requests because they feel entitled to receive the grade they want. I suspect their parents taught them the skill of making excuses with teachers and of not respecting the value a teacher can bring to the classroom.

If anybody, it's Christian parents who need to impart the truth that making excuses is a dead-end proposition. Jesus tells a parable in Luke 14:15–24 about a man hosting a party. Those who are invited but make excuses do not taste the man's dinner. Jesus is referring to the kingdom of heaven, and the excuse makers do not enter that glory. Of course, you as parents don't want your children to make excuses that keep them from the kingdom. Therefore, don't make excuses that diminish the authority of their Bible teachers. Instead trust your kids' Bible class teachers, and you will find them valuable allies in the quest to produce Christians who will rise to each new challenge.

Rosalind

Bible class teachers can be some of the most influential people in a child's life. Consequently, it is very important for teachers to be encouraging in educating and guiding children to love the Lord. I had a teacher who would ask open-ended, thought-provoking questions of the class. Students would give correct answers but not the particular answer the teacher was looking for. He would tell them they were wrong. How discouraging!

Situations like this can dampen students' enthusiasm and possibly deter them from participating in the future. Being a Bible class teacher myself, I understand that we are not necessarily professional teachers and that there may be no mechanism for critiquing our performance. I certainly don't want to discourage teachers but want to encourage us all to analyze our own effectiveness in the classroom.

Another scenario that I often saw as a child in Bible class was one where a few students did not participate and failed to prepare or complete assignments, and the teacher let it slide. If we had been in our secular school, the students would have failed the class. But sometimes it seems that because there are no grades or pass/fails in Bible class, it creates an easy way out of tasks for kids. The subjects learned in Bible class are vastly more important than those in everyday school. Be sure your students understand this. Hold them to a high standard.

Bible class teachers are with their students no more than a couple of hours a week, typically. Ideally, parents have the freedom to spend hours with their kids every day. Staying in tune with what is happening in the classroom and being in communication with your child's Bible class teacher prepares you to regularly review and reemphasize the lessons learned in class. Take opportunities at home and in everyday situations where the topics apply.

A friend grew up going to Bible class on a regular basis. He learned Bible stories and was taught vital information. But now, as an adult, he has trouble remembering lots of the things he knows he learned as a child. While he acknowledges that he should have put in more effort, he attributes this inability to remember in part to the fact that his parents did not discuss his Bible lessons at home with him. Teaching was left strictly to the Bible class teachers on Sunday. For example, if parents know that a recent lesson topic was compassion for others, they can put this into action during the week with their child and help the lesson have a practical application. The teachers are not around for those everyday situations, but if the parents and teachers work as a team, they can collectively point their children toward heaven.

Claire

Children would greatly benefit from parents reminding them to do their Bible lessons and reviewing the lessons with them before Bible class. Lessons should be a variety of activities: memorizing verses, reading passages, singing hymns, demonstrating the fruit of the Spirit, looking through a children's picture Bible, or completing a Bible study project. It is difficult to love someone if you don't know her or him. It is no different for children and the way they view God. Children love God more if they know God and if the adults in their lives demonstrate His ways to them.

You may be surprised how much a child can know. My friend Milton and his brother went to a dinner at someone's house after a gospel meeting. The group of about eighty people participated in a Bible trivia game. Milton and his brother (ten and twelve years old at the time) placed in the top three spots, competing against adults. One factor that may have led to their impressive performance is the rigorous Bible class they attended twice per week as children. Milton says that his teachers were careful to monitor his progress with Bible reading and memory verses and then to fill out a record confirming that the work was completed. The students and teachers took it very seriously. There was incentive to know God.

In one of my master's degree courses, a professor gave us an assignment to create a video about a company's supply chain. The effort on the video wouldn't be part of our grade. As you might guess, for this assignment students made some terrible videos, with my group's being just someone sitting in front of a camera boringly reading something that had been typed for him. In another class we also had a video project, but the results were much different—it was graded. The videos featured good editing, music, and special effects that came alive on-screen.

The videos remind me of something I noticed when I was once filling in to teach Bible class for a group of four- and five-year-olds. The first part of the class was a quick lesson. Throughout the lesson I asked questions about the information I had just shared. The results were dismal, with few to no hands being raised to recall something I had said just a minute before.

There was a very obvious shift when I wrote the students' names on the board and began awarding points for correct answers. Hands started shooting up immediately, and the kids truly listened to what I was saying in order to participate in the activity. The difference between the beginning of class and later in the class was that an incentive to learn had been introduced. It doesn't have to be a game; it could be a matching activity or a problem-solving exercise—something to keep their minds from passivity. Certainly, the most important reasons to pay attention in Bible class are to know God, to grow closer to God, and to glorify Him. But it is quite valuable to understand children's brains and what helps them to resist losing focus. Just like the adults in my supply chain class, these children had to have a good reason to pay attention to detail and learn about God.

Assignments

1. For parents, decide on one action you can start taking now to improve the teamwork between you and your child's Bible class teacher. Write it down, make a plan, and follow through.
2. For those without children in Bible class, decide on one action you can start taking now to support Bible classes. Write it down on a note and put the note in a conspicuous spot to remind you to follow through.
3. For Bible class teachers, name one action you can start taking to improve your communication with the parents of your students. Write it down on a note, plan how to carry out your action, and then follow through.

Chapter 9 Discussion Questions

1. The ultimate responsibility for teaching children about God and His Son rests with parents. They can, however, use the knowledge and expertise of Bible class teachers to great advantage. Name some ways you take opportunities to encourage and work with teachers to make sure your children get the benefits of their teaching. What are the advantages of your staying in tune with and apprised of what is happening in the classroom? How important is it to you to stay in touch with their Bible class teachers? Explain your answer.
2. Teachers and parents can be a united force. How involved are you with your kids' teachers as to classroom activities? Do you ask how your children are doing in Bible class? Be sure you present a united front with the teacher—kids will know if this is not the case. What can you do to prepare your child for a more effective learning experience? Consider the example of Carrie (chapter 3) and her Saturday night training. Do you make sure your kids get a good night's sleep on Saturday and

a nutritious Sunday breakfast so that they are mentally prepared and alert to participate in the lesson?

3. Give some thought to the subject of discipline in the classroom. Is it best if the teacher and child can work out disciplinary problems together? When should parents be alerted? If brought to the parents' attention, do you think you could be objective in dealing with the situation? How would this affect future teacher-parent-child relationships? As a Christian be mindful of what your attitude should be.
4. Why do people make excuses? How often do you make excuses for your children? What do kids learn from this habit? In what ways can this affect their future lives, both spiritually and socially?
5. How do you feel about rewarding students (awarding points, other incentives) to give them a reason to pay attention and learn about God? Should this procedure be limited to certain age groups? Are today's kids being taught to be too competitive? What other reasons do you give your kids for the need to learn about God?

For Personal Use

Write down the most important concept you gained from chapter 9 in regard to developing spiritual determination in kids. You will be asked to do this for each chapter. Then personally review your answers at the conclusion of this twelve-lesson study. What did you learn about yourself? What can you pass on to the next generation? Hopefully, this will have been a profitable study for you.

10

PEOPLE WILL DO ANYTHING FOR A FREE T-SHIRT

Colleen

I used to work for an organization that operated conferences for professionals. My boss, Ray, a retired engineer, was learning new things about the world of marketing. One time we were discussing giveaway items to provide for our conference attendees. He marveled, "People will do anything for a free T-shirt." At first I just laughed, but as the decades have worn on, I see the serious kink in us human beings that makes this a glistening piece of wisdom. We *will* do anything for one.

In our rational moments, we see perfectly God's way to heaven, and we commit to obey Him. But over time physical distractions beckon more and more forcefully. For many, bodily cravings, demands from peers, and even free T-shirts topple both the novice and the experienced. Jesus's Parable of the Sower hovers imposingly, with its caution about the cares and riches of this life and their choke hold on the human race (Matthew 13:22). We can all probably say we've been guilty to some extent and have witnessed Christians who traded eternity for something of relatively scant value. Some people are under tremendous pressure until Satan finally wins, some frivolously choose a prize to the neglect of Christ, and on occasion people are duped because they are just not too swift on the uptake.

Some people are under tremendous pressure. We know what preys on Jesus's mind the most by examining His last discourses before the crucifixion (John 16:31–17:26). In the garden just before His arrest, Jesus warns the disciples that they will be persecuted so that their belief will dissipate and they will abandon Him. He prays to God to perpetuate the unity they share at that moment. In the next scene, He is taken into custody, and His friends all run for their lives. Those who choose the same exit today are in good company but still selling their souls.

When Christians' lives, family relationships, finances, etc. are threatened, it becomes an intense scrutiny of their loyalty: God or the world? Jesus tells His disciples, "Go your way; behold, I send you out as lambs among wolves" (Luke 10:3). The prospect is a gory one, but He doesn't call them to shelter. He urges them to march on. The key is that He has prepared them with training and specific instructions to arm them. It is the same with us and, in turn, as we send out our children.

Some frivolously choose a prize. They know exactly what they're doing, but they give in anyway. A Christian friend and I discussed the ups and downs of trying to find a godly marriage partner. She mentioned single Christians she has known who dated those who were not committed to the Lord. She remarked that "they compromise a lot." They sell out in order to win a beautiful or rich or charming mate. They might try to convert that boyfriend or girlfriend, but when it doesn't happen, they don't have a plan B. They merely keep dating the person, marry him or her, and raise children in a wobbly religious environment.

In other cases the prize may be a legitimate pursuit, such as housekeeping, feeding your family, or keeping up with the daily news that is given priority over Christian relationships and activities. I had a talk with an older Christian one time who was no longer affiliating herself with the church. She spoke of her history with the Lord's people and mentioned her father's work as a leader in the church. As I was leaving, I told her that I hoped she would come to services later that evening. She begged off because she was having a big-screen TV delivered then. I advised that she needed to decide which was more important. She said, "If you were having a big-screen TV delivered, wouldn't you say that was important?" Her sentiment didn't shock me as much as her willingness to be so candid with her logic.

Some are just not too swift on the uptake. We might be able to picture our sweet little infant as a harmless dove but never a wise serpent. However, Jesus wants him to be both, according to Matthew 10:16: "Behold, I send you out as sheep in the midst of wolves. Therefore be wise as serpents and harmless as doves." This is one area where trusting children need parents and other adults who are on the ball. When children grow up in Christian homes, they probably won't be on guard for the cruel tricks kids play on each other. I grew up with children who tricked me into doing things that were wrong or that made me look like a buffoon. A generation later I was determined to clue my children in on ill-treatment and other deceit by their friends that had gone unrecognized.

God doesn't want any of His people to be naive, and it's no excuse for foolish choices. Of the Pharisees Jesus said, "Let them alone. They are blind leaders of the blind. And if the blind leads the blind, both will fall into a ditch" (Matthew 15:14). Those who lead in sin and those who follow receive the same punishment in this case. Vigilant and shrewd parents provide education and protection so that kids at all stages are quick on the uptake, defeating the world's fraud.

Scammed Old-Lady Style

My friend lamented, "I fell for an old lady scam!" She had been sick and home from work when she got a phone call. The caller ID showed the name of her bank, so she answered and had a conversation with a man concerning her checking account. He said someone had tried to access funds from this account. The man sounded professional. This gained her trust. He also told her he was sorry she was sick and hated to have to deliver this alarming news. This gained her good will.

The man stated several pieces of information from my friend's financial records and said he needed one more number so that he could access the account to secure it. My friend gave him the number. The two said, "Goodbye," and the call ended.

Just after hanging up, my friend received a call from her bank. This time the bank employee really did work for her bank and had the authority to inform her that all her money had just been withdrawn from her checking account. Scammed!

How did she fall? The crook used the words we're warned about in the Bible, flattering and eloquent. He told her there was a problem, which alarmed her, and right away he relieved her by saying he was going to help. Then he made quick friends with her by being a man who actually cared that she was sick.

Being tricked doesn't affect just the one who falls for the scam; it affects others indirectly. Fortunately, my friend didn't keep a lot of money in her checking account, and bank insurance covered her loss, but banks pay for that insurance. They and their insurance policies will continue to compensate for the crimes of the thief on the phone and the naivete of those scammed.

Transfer these lessons to the innocent who fall for the old "wolf in sheep's clothing" bit. Their souls are lost in a direct way, and what about the collateral damage? These include children who see their parents and other role models pursuing sin, married people whose lives are turned upside down by an unfaithful husband or wife, and people at work who observe the behavior of Christians who have been tricked into speaking or acting in ways that are condemned by God.

This calls for the defense of our children's souls as we stand strong in the noise of conflict to uphold the principles and standards we confirmed during peacetime. I'm not talking about fighting your children's struggles with their teachers and other kids. This is about defending the broad, long-term goals. It certainly entails teaching them how to contend with others and even advocate for themselves, but it goes way deeper than this world's daily disappointments.

A Few Practical Strategies

The apostle Peter warns us to "Be sober, be vigilant; because your adversary the devil walks about like a roaring lion, seeking whom he may devour" (1 Peter 5:8). Satan is on duty with this intent around the clock. Therefore, our kids should be without vulnerabilities. Here are some ways to see to it:

1. Build in your young ones the ability to read analytically and form an understanding of the scriptures on their own instead of just accepting your take.
2. Teach them hermeneutics in order to figure out how to apply various passages as either direct commands, necessary inferences, approved apostolic examples, etc.
3. Teach them to consider other related verses and to work through arguments logically.

In the same way that young readers learn phonics to be able to figure out any new word, your children can get under the hood on any biblical passage and decide how to comprehend and apply it correctly. It is God's word becoming their word.

When we equip children with the tools to do their own analysis, they are less likely to blindly follow the opinions and errors of others than if teachers merely lecture. With Bible reading, to leave children passive in the exercise while we simply tell them how to apply scripture is more shallow and less empowering. Teach children not to need an answer of biblical import right away but to research it and get a full answer. Don't only ask a preacher or parent. Fallible human beings may give a wrong explanation or a narrow one.

Which is easier to trade for the world's trinkets? A belief children have worked for and embraced through their own diligence or a belief handed to them by their childhood authorities? With each session of study with you, each encouragement to be disciplined and think as individuals, the temptation of the free T-shirt grows more and more impotent, until it is exposed as the puny fake that it is.

Haley

There is no innate evil in a free T-shirt. The problem lies in the decision-making of the receiver of the shirt. Suppose you're at a basketball game and staring the T-shirt cannon down its barrel, hoping one of its missiles will come your way. A T-shirt lands in your lap, to the disappointment of everyone in your section. You take your spoils home, place it in the shirt drawer of your dresser, and whatever the final score of the basketball game, you won.

On the next Saturday, you're looking for something casual to wear, and you choose the free T-shirt, because it's new and it makes you feel like a winner. As soon as someone sees you wearing it, you are a walking advertising campaign for the local cable provider. The local cable provider is paying you nothing, yet you willingly spread the word about it to everyone who sees you wear its ad.

Hopefully, you were thoughtful about your decision to advertise, but in truth most people wouldn't make a conscious decision to work for the local cable provider for free. The problem with the free T-shirt is that it makes it very easy for the recipient to leave the decision to someone else. It's easy for this lax decision-making to infiltrate our lives. When we stop being vigilant and making decisions for ourselves, we cease to be the wise and discerning disciples Christ wants. That's why it's of great importance that parents teach their children to be conscious of each decision they make.

In a book called *Nudge* by Cass Sunstein and Richard Thaler, a Nobel Laureate in economics, the authors write about how we make decisions. Every move we make is a decision, but that doesn't necessarily mean we have consciously decided and thought about the consequences of it. In many cases the decisions we make are the result of nudges from outside ourselves. The authors cite an example from research into college students' study habits. Students who share a room with vigilant studiers have higher grades, and students who share with slackers have lower ones (Sunstein 2008).

Of course, we know that who we consciously choose to spend time with will affect us. The Bible says in Proverbs 13:20, "He who walks with wise men will be wise, But the companion of fools will be destroyed." The scary thing is that others end up affecting our decisions—such as whether to spend time studying or recreating—more than we realize.

To steer your children away from thoughtless decision-making, do these two things:

1. Make sure they know how easily their decisions can be influenced by others.
2. Teach them to be confident people who can withstand peers' and Satan's pressure and trust their own good judgment.

If we teach our kids to recognize when others—the local cable provider, a roommate, or the devil—are making decisions for them and to be confident to trust their own decisions, they will be conscious decision makers. We will have taught them to be conscious Christians.

Rosalind

Luke describes how Jesus goes on a walk one day and tells a man, "Follow me" (Luke 9:59). The man replies that he needs to go bury his father first, but Christ tells him to leave that desire behind and go proclaim God's word. Concern about burying a family member is no doubt a respectable thing, but you cannot let it hold you back from doing the work of the Lord. Put yourself in that man's shoes. Maybe for you it is, "Lord, first let me get my kids through high school," or, "Lord, first let me become financially stable."

On the same walk, another man volunteers that he will follow Christ, but he wants to go back and say goodbye to his family first. Again it seems reasonable that this man would want to see his family before leaving, maybe leaving permanently. Jesus responds, "No one, having put his hand to the plow, and looking back, is fit for the kingdom of God" (Luke 9:62). If the man went back to say goodbye to his family, the concern is that he would have second thoughts.

My family appreciates a good episode of *The Andy Griffith Show.* One of our favorites is the one in which Barney Fife buys a car. A little old lady named Mrs. Lesh shows up with a shiny car she says belonged to her late husband. Barney is sucked into the story she tells of how much the car meant to her husband and how difficult it is for her to part with it. Barney hastily makes the overpriced purchase, believing it to be too good to be true. As the woman is walking away, she stops dramatically to turn back for one last emotional look at the car. Barney yells to her not to look back (Fritzell 1999).

If you are a fan of *The Andy Griffith Show,* you know that Mrs. Lesh is a sneaky con woman who sells Barney a lemon of a car. But he believes the car is of great importance to this woman. If she looks back, she might change her mind, being pulled back to an object of seemingly high importance to her. In the same way, Jesus tells the man in Luke chapter 9 not to look back to things of his earthly life, because they can so quickly make us change our minds and retreat from service to God.

Jesus is not asking that we neglect our family members and weighty matters of this world but that we beware of the physical distractions Satan puts right in our path. Our salvation and the salvation of our children are not worth trading for a frivolous earthly reward or satisfaction.

Claire

In Acts chapter 5, the apostles are beaten by order of the council because they preached Christ. The punishment is meant to stop the apostles, but instead they rejoice and are emboldened to preach some more. Why? They had invested themselves in the work commanded by Jesus. One of the best ways to keep Christians from being drawn toward free T-shirts is to help them build a vested interest in the work in Christ's kingdom. Sometimes people start to sell out on being faithful Christians because they feel their talents aren't needed in the church. This can set them up to seek that sense of joy somewhere else.

There are always plenty of opportunities to use our talents to serve God and His people, but we need the discipline to take those opportunities. However, sometimes even when we offer, we get turned down in our efforts to help. This can be especially damaging to children who have zeal for being helpers.

I remember being discouraged in this way myself. When I was younger, I offered to help someone at church with a big project. Sadly, the person didn't take me up on that offer, not even to do a small or simple task. Maybe a kid seemed like more of a hindrance in getting things done, and maybe I would have been. But I beg to say it was an opportunity the adult shouldn't have let pass. It was a chance to let a little girl learn what it means to be of service to others.

To me as a child, it was a big deal to even offer my help. I was sad when I realized later that the person had completed the project without me. Perhaps it was an honest mistake and the person had forgotten about my offer. But that's part of my point: we must be diligent anytime there is an opportunity to be part of a teaching moment with a child. It could have a lasting negative or positive effect. That positive effect can strengthen allegiance to Christ and His people.

Once, at a small group meeting with church members, a person announced that donations were needed for a special cause. I had a paying job, saw it was an effort I would like to support, and gave some money right then. Later the person tried to give the money back to me. I refused it, citing that I had given it because I really wanted to help. After an awkward exchange, the person finally accepted the money.

I felt embarrassed. I guess the person assumed I couldn't afford it and that it was not expected of me as a younger member. That is where we go wrong sometimes. There are certain people with handicaps or barriers of sickness, old age, youth, and many other factors, and less is demanded of them. However, we all need to find ways to do good no matter our circumstances. When we try to hold back Christians (even graciously) from what they have found to do, it can lead them to feel their contributions aren't really important or that those contributions are not needed by others. For every Christian, the more we have invested time and other resources in the cause of Christ, the less likely we are to turn our heads to the world's enticements.

Assignments

1. Answer and discuss with a partner or class the questions below.
2. Recite Luke 4:1–14 from memory. If you already had it memorized, have you gotten rusty? Work out any kinks in your delivery.

Chapter 10 Discussion Questions

1. How can we hold to our commitment to God and not allow distractions of the cares and riches of this life to intervene? This chapter presents three categories of people who sell out to temptations and trade eternity for something of little value. Do you know of people who have faced similar situations? What was the outcome? Did they ever take steps to correct their bad judgment? Was their faith weakened or made stronger by this subsequent decision?
2. Apply the practical strategies to your present method of teaching your kids. Are you showing them how to do their own analysis of scripture, or are they accepting the word of the teacher? Why is this so important? (Note: Think of the value of this kind of training when unscriptural innovations threaten the church.)
3. Haley deals extensively with decision-making and the importance of parents teaching their children to be conscious of this process. Are you aware of how much influence other people (peers or adults) may have on your kids? Are you comfortable with your kids' choice of friends, who could be exerting pressure on them or making decisions for them? If not, how would you handle this problem?
4. From Luke chapter 9:59–62 Rosalind recounts the story of two men who put care for their families above following Jesus. These men face a turning point in their lives. Do they make the right choice? Sometimes decisions must be made on the

spot. We may not have time to ponder the possible choices—there will be only one and an alternative. How do you teach your children the necessity of looking past physical distractions and considering the consequences of each decision they make? When should this instruction begin?

5. (a) In Claire's section of this chapter, she addresses two accounts where a young person offered to help with a project but was turned down and the resulting feeling of discouragement. What counsel would you have given if this were your child?
   (b) Why is it so important that we all use every teaching opportunity with a child? As older Christians we must realize that, by what we teach and by our example, we are preparing younger members to be the church of tomorrow. Is this a terrifying responsibility to you?
   (c) When we become Christians, we make a commitment to serve God for the rest of our lives. This includes old, young, sick, handicapped, etc. What are some ways in which those who may be limited can do good works? What can you do to help them?

For Personal Use

Write down the most important concept you gained from chapter 10 in regard to developing spiritual grit in families. You will be asked to do this for each chapter. Then personally review your answers at the conclusion of this twelve-lesson study. What did you learn about yourself? What can you pass on to the next generation? Hopefully, this will have been a profitable study for you.

11

WHEN WE FEEL LIKE GIVING UP

Colleen

When is it time to give up on a soul? Never. I could stop there, but let's develop this answer.

To never give up is a state of mind we must nurture in ourselves if we are to see our children through to their spiritual and earthly potential. They're under construction, and even exemplary children ride their ups and downs. Many toddlers, young girls and boys, teenagers, and grown children can be a challenge to their parents. It takes tenacious fingernails to hang on when efforts seem to bring no results and there appears no stable foothold in the dark. When you feel like giving up, buttress your high standards and don't surrender.

All Alone and Beaten to a Pulp

Last year my daughters and I went tubing on a river in North Carolina. I pictured a peaceful, lazy float, not one like my previous whitewater rafting experience when we tipped in rapids. What could go wrong with tubing? I thought. Kids were doing it, no helmet required. Immediately upon launch my tube flipped me into the seemingly gentle rapids and abandoned me. I lost my hat. I was dashed across rocks and carried downstream, unable to stop myself.

My daughters rescued my tube and hat and brought them back to me once we were in calm water. I could barely touch bottom, so the only way I could get back onto my tube was for some kind stranger to hoist me up. How embarrassing.

As I drifted with the current, I examined several cuts and bruises from the rough embarkation. My pride was also kicked around, because everybody else seemed to be piloting their tubes just fine, enjoying the gliding ride. Each time I approached a new set of small rapids, I braced—afraid to flip again. When we completed the route, I couldn't get out of that river fast enough. My kids were eager to go it another time, which was the last thing I would consider. As I waited for them, I was perplexed at why I had been such a poor tuber. Was I out of shape and uncoordinated? Old and unwieldy?

The girls finally finished their second float down the river, and I met them as they emerged from the water. I was sure they would want to tube it again, and I asked them. Get this—they said emphatically, "No!"

Why? The second time down the river, they had tipped and endured the same indignity and wounds that I did the first time. Hard knocks make us many things, and one of them is humiliated.

Just like with my tubing adventure, when life is going badly for us in some endeavor, it can be even more rankling if everybody else seems to be finding success, having an easy time. I have seen plenty of parents who appear to be doing all the right things, but their children cause trouble and heartache at various stages of their development. I have seen parents who made big mistakes in rearing their children, and the kids turn out exemplary. There are all manner of situations in between. When things aren't going well with your children, the plan of action is the same as in all areas of the faithful walk: keep the long time perspective in sight. Continue to do what you can to optimize the situation, insisting on upholding the high standard of God.

Insight from a Christian Mother

I interviewed a Christian mother who has weathered several challenges with her children. I can't say it any better, so here is what she wrote and contributed to this book:

Now, unless your field of education is in child development or child psychology, where you know what to do in any given situation—how to act, how to react, and what to expect—then I believe most parents learn and grow as they are raising their children. Not too many parents have it all figured out before they have kids. Parenting will expose strengths and weaknesses you were not aware of.

Parenting can be challenging, but it is even more so in the following situations:

1. You have or your child has a disability.
2. You have a bad spouse or no spouse.
3. You are parenting an adult child.
4. You are parenting a grandchild.

There are many other extra challenges, none of which is an excuse not to parent. It is a matter of figuring out what is necessary, possibly getting help, taking one day at a time, doing what is needful—and pray, pray, pray.

In the case of my husband and me, we are still trying to parent an adult daughter and be parents to her daughter. Our adult child has had the opportunity to make good choices in her life; she didn't always do that. Now she must live with the consequences of her choices and try to make corrections. Our job with her is to support current good decisions and try not to enable bad ones. However, our focus and priorities must be for the benefit of our granddaughter, because unlike her mother, she is still a child who needs guidance and protection.

Here are some of the differences in being a grandparent versus being a parent:

1. We have exchanged the energy of youth for (hopefully) wisdom and life experience.
2. We are more capable of seeing life through the child's eyes—slowing down and enjoying it.
3. We can see more of the big picture, have a greater appreciation for mortality, and are better equipped to make good decisions and to prioritize.

Part of the difficulty, or lack of it, in raising a grandchild lies in what type of person he or she is. Is she stubborn or cooperative? Is he spiritually minded, or is there a fight over every restraint put on him? Does she enjoy doing and learning new things, or is she lazy? My grandchild's personality will make my job easier or harder. But either way I have been given this opportunity, this responsibility, and I must fulfill it to the best of my ability. I must view it as a blessing—a blessing for us to have her and a blessing for her to have us.

I would be remiss if I did not mention life from the grandchild's viewpoint. First, if a parent is still in the grandchild's life, it is sometimes difficult for her to know who is in authority. We have had to be firm with her mother about some of the more serious, consequential things. Some of the lesser things we deal with on an ongoing basis are: bedtime routine, meals and snacks, watching too much TV, going places locally or long trips, appropriate clothing, fake tattoos, weird nail polish, etc. We disagree with our daughter on some of these issues.

Second, my granddaughter knows what a family is supposed to be, and it is difficult for her to see her friends have a "normal" family when she does not. They live with mom and dad, they go on vacation with mom and dad, and they share pictures of their family and talk about all they do. We told her we are her parents (for all intents and purposes), and she should feel free to share what we do together and not be concerned that we are grandparents and not parents. We do similar things with her as other families and try to make her life as normal as possible.

Third, my granddaughter lost everything she owned in a fire. She occasionally talks about something she doesn't have anymore that "was lost in the fire," and she cries (not just for that item but for the whole bad experience). That's okay to feel a loss and express it, but then we tell her that it's just stuff. There are people far worse off than she is, and she has so many other blessings, like the home she lives in with people who love her, her church family, her extended family, her school, all her friends, and of course God Himself, who is the greatest source of blessing and comfort.

Colleen

The above "Insight from a Christian Mother" doesn't use the phrase "problem solver," but the idea is woven throughout her discourse, and that is exactly what she is. When parents develop themselves to be problem solvers, they are strengthened and less likely to give up—even in the face of certain defeat, when sound reasoning says, "surrender." In his book *The Joy of Growing Old in Christ,* Dee Bowman reflects, "One of the most dastardly implements of the Devil is his temptation of us to quit too early. He plants discouragement, sows doubts and seeks mental compromises. How many plans were thwarted because someone stopped too soon?" (Bowman 2019). Indeed, most if not all parents have experienced discouragement, doubt, and compromise when leading their offspring. Recognizing early in the game that these are merely Satan's tools gives us the broad view of the situation and supplies us with the cunning to fight back with resolution and solutions.

Up Against a Dread Disease

In 1970 my family knew a little boy who awoke in the middle of the night with a bat biting his thumb and digging in. The boy screamed, and his parents came running. According to the *Lima News* [Ohio], several days later the bat was confirmed rabid, and a doctor started serum injections on the victim (Krumel 2018). Unfortunately, it was too late to prevent the boy from contracting rabies, a full-blown case.

He dropped into a semi coma. There was no documented evidence of anyone's ever surviving the infectious disease; the boy was as good as dead in the eyes of the medical world and history.

They could have resigned themselves to making the patient comfortable and awaiting the inevitable, but three doctors and the Atlanta Center for Disease Control would not quit. They took up an offensive strategy to simply treat and conquer individual symptoms as they appeared. For example, when the boy's "heart and breathing began to rapidly increase, the doctors quickly did a tracheotomy. When his left hand began opening and closing, they administered anti-convulsant medications. No antibiotics or steroids were used," according to the newspaper article.

Over the next two months, the boy gradually improved and was released from the hospital. He and the medical team had smashed an unbeatable affliction, making this boy the first person ever to survive a case of rabies. Problem solvers saved a doomed child's life. With the same attitude, parents of children who are spiritually on the wrong path must be problem solvers and teach their kids to be so. If that skill is already sharp before trouble comes, it can bring about a rescue.

To Be Problem Solvers

In my work with producing training game simulations, a major difference between testing novices and testing experienced users is level of normalcy in the assessment. For novices the questions or simulations deal with performing operations as they are intended to work. For experienced users the assessments focus on problem-solving. The worth of these students is measured by their ability to devise what to do if something's wrong. They get paid more money, because experience plus perseverance resolves difficulties. The people most valuable to a company or family or a church—are the problem solvers. They'll always be the indispensable ones.

This is a major plank in the platform of building spiritual grit in yourself and then dispensing it to your boys and girls. Cultivating a perseverant way of approaching life brings children along as people who figure out what to do. We need them. There are plenty who will perform as they're told; they may even do an above average job. But when the wheels fall off, work stops. There are a few who may be willing to troubleshoot. Beyond that there are one or two who get ready to craft a strategy for the next problem even before it materializes. The church suffers without these solutions drivers. You and I must develop such people.

Bible students who are eight or nine years old do pretty well at memorizing facts and plots. They are interested in drawing conclusions and making applications, but most are just getting their feet wet at it. When asked, "Why would Peter deny that he knew Jesus?" only a rare one at this age can give a reasonable guess.

I had a student one time who was a natural problem solver. When I asked the class a thought question, the other kids might reflect for a couple of seconds and then defer to the class mastermind. He didn't always have a good answer, but he did use a viable method. He took time to think and then threw out a couple of guesses. The key to this exercise is that he wasn't afraid to be wrong as he narrowed down his guesses to the most likely. He left a warm place in my heart, but I'm concerned that the other kids weren't up to the task. They gave up.

It occurs to me that when teenage and adult children continue to follow the wrong path in life, perhaps it is not apathy or lack of self-control but their inability to solve their own problems that perpetuates failures in life. These individuals probably recognize and disdain their bad decisions and status. However, they are not adept at outlining a solution and then sticking to it. They keep themselves behind the eight ball of their own volition. This goes for all of us at one time or another. In these pinch times, don't throw in the towel; keep gathering information and continue to think out your plan of attack.

Haley

When the economy is in a downturn or you are worried about the future of your job, you prepare for difficulties that may come. You save, budget, and cut down on unnecessary spending—no question about it. These actions build you to be fortified against financial uncertainty in the future. When the stock market is strong and things are going smoothly at work, however, many people tend to loosen up their finances and forget that the future may hold something other than safety. This pattern of tightness and laxness can manifest itself in the parenting realm as well.

When there's an opioid epidemic staring them in the face, parents make bold efforts to secure a future for their children that is independent of substances. They do everything they can to make them discerning about navigating the decisions that lead to drug problems. Their children become strong to face this type of temptation. The tricky thing is that we don't know what the future holds, and if some unforeseen evil tempts your children, you want them to be judicious in all ways so they're prepared to resist.

Consider a family I know. The first generation raised their children in a time and place where the culture supported wholesome Christian living. It was easy to raise Christians in an environment like this. The second generation grew up, and its members were good people with stable marriages. They raised their children to go to church and be good people, the same way their parents had, but no longer did the culture support this.

The second generation raised their kids to be nice but not to be savvy. When members of the third generation grew up, they didn't have the backing of a society that frowned on worldly behavior and lax morals, nor did they have the keen insight to resist a temptation that their parents and grandparents had never conceived to be a problem. The third generation is now a group of people facing marital troubles and a weak faith in God. They didn't learn to be shrewd when they were young, so they encountered consequences later.

The first generation would certainly have raised a shrewd second generation if they had imagined that the future could be a difficult one to navigate as Christians. Instead they fell prey to the feeling of safety that comes with living in a wholesome time, place, and culture. They gave up on teaching their children to be tough spiritually, because it didn't seem necessary at the time. They didn't keep their eyes on the horizon.

We know that we shouldn't give up on our children when things are challenging. As Christians we push them to be tenacious and face what is difficult. But it is just as important not to give up on our children when things are easy. In 2 Corinthians 2, Paul warns us not to let Satan take advantage of us, because he will take every opportunity. The key as parents is not to give up on building courage and determination in your children—even in seasons of relative safety—so that their spiritual acumen keeps the devil at bay.

Rosalind

Can you think of someone who, despite your poor behavior or character, never gave up on you? A teacher, friend, coach, uncle, or grandmother? I can. And I hate to think of where I would be without his or her perseverance with me.

"Insight from a Christian Mother" emphasizes the importance of a network in a child's life, even if the network is different from what you ever thought it might be. Consider the redwood forests. These trees are some of the tallest trees in the whole world, reaching heights of three hundred feet or higher. But their roots are actually very shallow, typically only a few feet deep. A redwood tree gains strength and fortitude by intertwining its roots with those of the trees around it; the roots can fuse together too. This network of roots protects the trees and allows them to withstand wind, rain, and other acts of nature. Children need this same type of support system and to know that you are rooted in Christ and so are they. When kids start to falter, their team, whoever that may be, needs to be there, keeping them standing tall.

This willingness to endure is exemplified precisely in the relationship between Jesus and His apostles. For approximately three years, the Rabbi and His disciples talk, walk, eat, and travel together. Jesus explains His earthly work and its principles, including the purpose to consider heaven home and Earth enemy territory. Just before His arrest and as they look on, He prays about His disciples to the Father, "I have given them Your word; and the world has hated them because they are not of the world, just as I am not of the world" (John 17:14). Yet as He is taken into custody, Peter attacks with the world's implement of war—a sword. Then all the apostles flee. Does Jesus disown them? No.

After Jesus's resurrection, for forty days He speaks to them of "the things pertaining to the kingdom of God" (Acts 1:3). Apparently they don't comprehend, because the disciples' last question to Him is, "Lord, will You at this time restore the kingdom to Israel?" (Acts 1:6). Jesus doesn't abandon them but continues with His mission, never wavering on their serious role in it. Then on the Day of Pentecost, all the fog dissipates and the light takes over. The Holy Spirit descends, and the twelve are empowered, emboldened, and clad in the spiritual armor Jesus watched for during their years together (see Acts 2). They're standing tall and willing to die for the cause of Christ.

Considering Jesus in this example, let's not give up on anyone. It could be that you are not the parent but are watching parents lose heart concerning the salvation of a child. You can be the friend who refuses to let go of this precious soul. Maybe you are a child who refuses to give up on your parents. I know young adults with unfaithful parents who feel the same distress as a parent with a wayward child, hoping for a change. Just remember the unfailing love God shows for you and never give up on the return of your loved ones.

Claire

In the Old Testament, two examples, the young shepherd David and Esther's cousin Mordecai, don't know when to give up. They know only that they can't give up. Under extreme pressure, the two do not take the easy road. Backing down or compromising would have been disastrous for their people, and both understand that God's side always prevails.

In 1 Samuel 17, David brings food to his brothers, who are helping to battle the Philistines and the giant, Goliath. One brother mocks David for saying that Goliath's being defeated with God's help is a done deal. David "turned from him toward another and said the same thing; and these people answered him as the first ones did" (1 Samuel 17:30). Just like we do sometimes, David looks to others to find reassurance, but there is none, because no one has faith in God like David. This young shepherd knows that God will defeat Goliath by his hand, accomplishing a task that all of Israel thinks impossible. David does not quit, even when all of Israel has quit.

Neither does Mordecai surrender. For at least a year, he is at the king's gate to make sure Esther is well. His persistence there incidentally leads to discovering a plot to murder King Ahasuerus. Furthermore, Mordecai does not bow to Haman, a man of significant status in the kingdom. Haman is so furious that he wants to murder all the Jewish people.

Haman's wrath doesn't stop Mordecai; he is willing to risk his life in attempting to thwart Haman's plan. Neither is Esther's reluctance to seek help from the king any match for Mordecai's determination. He tells her, "Do not think in your heart that you will escape in the king's palace any more than all the other Jews. For if you remain completely silent at this time, relief and deliverance will arise for the Jews from another place, but you and your father's house will perish. Yet who knows whether you have come to the kingdom for such a time as this?" (Esther 4:13–14). In the end, Mordecai's devotion and determination to expend all means before giving up saves the lives of both the king and God's people.

Just like David and Mordecai, we can be people who never concede defeat. Both exhibited this attitude not only in their words but also in their actions. Children are ready to be influenced by the courageous words and actions of those who are older and have experience in life. How reliable will we be in rising to what they need and the example they are waiting for?

Assignments

1. Reflect on Luke 4:1–14 that's been assigned to recite from memory. Note at least one way Jesus keeps from giving in to Satan's temptations in this passage. How did Jesus answer Satan's attacks?

Chapter 11 Discussion Questions

1. Have you ever considered giving up on someone—maybe even yourself? This book has been building on the need for perseverance: to hang on, stay tough, and stand firm through all kinds of troubles. Chapter 2 describes the most important body part as the "backbone." Give examples of how establishing this mindset can get you through the tough times to reach long-term rewards. How do you explain this to your children so that they see the value of "keeping on keeping on?"
2. What is your view of the strategies stated in "Insight from a Christian Mother?" Do you approve of the methods she is using for her particular situation? Do you agree that the focus and priorities should be on the grandchild? What would you do to encourage her?
3. Problem-solving is a major plank in the platform of building spiritual fortitude in yourself and then dispensing it to your children. Some kids may find this more of a challenge than others. What steps would you take to motivate your child to develop a troubleshooting ability and not give up?
4. An interesting family history is given in Haley's narration of three generations who did not prepare for the future. This involved cultural differences in the lifestyles of each group that had not been taken into account in the teaching by the parents. What could have prevented these differences from having a negative effect on their faith? When the Israelites were entering into the land they were to possess—certainly

a foreign culture—Moses instructed them when they were to teach their children: sitting in the house, walking by the way, lying down, and arising (Deuteronomy 6:7; refer to chapter 5). What can we learn from this?

5. Do you have a support system enveloping your children and reinforcing the teaching you give them? Describe the network of consistency in your child's life. We've talked about Bible class teachers. Who else do you rely on—grandparents, aunts and uncles, friends? Here is where parents can have help with the daily gentle nudge: those who have your child's best interests in mind can be valuable allies by their association with him or her in teaching, encouraging, and strengthening your child to persevere.
6. What are some reasons that people give up? Why did David not give up? What did Mordecai do to reverse the king's order and allow God's people to overpower those who hated them? Was this good problem-solving? What is the lesson for us from these two stories?

For Personal Use

Write down the most important concept you gained from chapter 11 in regard to developing spiritual grit in families. You will be asked to do this for each chapter. Then personally review your answers at the conclusion of this twelve-lesson study. What did you learn about yourself? What can you pass on to the next generation? Hopefully, this will have been a profitable study for you.

12

A TOAST TO SUCCESS

Colleen

You wouldn't think this is actually a problem, but experts in the area of willpower and self-discipline advise about people who are so good at putting off gratification and attaining prosperity that they never celebrate success. They just continue to work, work, work. Come to think of it, I have been guilty of this with myself and my family, maybe even with coworkers. I have also been the victim of it. Amid all this willpower and reaching for future godly fulfillment, let's all make sure we come up for air every so often to look around and voice our gratefulness for what the children in our charge have actualized.

Note What's in the Quiver

This exercise is like taking inventory of your spiritual ammunition—it manifests confidence in facing the world each day and the future's uncertain horizon. Psalm 127 voices the role children play in pointing our exhilaration and dependence back to God in every single aspect of life:

> Unless the Lord builds the house,
> They labor in vain who build it;
> Unless the Lord guards the city,

The watchman stays awake in vain.
It is vain for you to rise up early,
To sit up late,
To eat the bread of sorrows;
For so He gives His beloved sleep.

Behold, children are a heritage from the Lord,
The fruit of the womb is a reward.
Like arrows in the hand of a warrior,
So are the children of one's youth.
Happy is the man who has his quiver full of them;
They shall not be ashamed,
But shall speak with their enemies in the gate.

Arrows win battles. The more you have, the higher your confidence and the better your chances of victory and advancement. The quality of the arrows matters, too, because accuracy and speed strongly influence their effectiveness. For instance, the fletching (feathers) steers your arrows cleanly through the air, so it must be maintained and set at the correct degree of turn. At the other end, a serious archer grinds down the tips to a super-sharp edge so that when shot, the arrows punch the holes intended.

The Bible is loaded with examples of girls and boys who behave with merit and influence the course of events, hitting the mark with precision and potency. Joseph, David, and Daniel get a lot of press; others not so much. Think of Miriam, who sticks around to keep an eye on her baby brother, Moses, after their mother hides him at the riverside (see Exodus 2). When royalty discovers the infant, Miriam assertively addresses Pharaoh's daughter with a clever offer of the perfect wet nurse, thus returning Moses to his mother's care for a time. Later Miriam is a prophetess and leads the women of Israel in a victory celebration praising God. Miriam adds to Jochebed and Amram's full quiver.

Another girl's parents are not named, but a young Israelite captive in 2 Kings 5 must have benefited from their training, because she shows mature selflessness and charity under extreme circumstances. This is the story of Naaman, the leper. A little girl rounded up in a Syrian raid on Israel is now a slave in a foreign country, serving Naaman's wife. This girl could have been bitter and vindictive in her displacement. She could have been immersed in resentment and withheld helpful information from Naaman, but she acts with beneficence when she offers to her captor, "If only my master were with the prophet who is in Samaria! For he would heal him of his leprosy" (2 Kings 5:3). Subsequently, the prophet Elisha delivers a complete recovery to Naaman.

By the slave girl's advice, the mighty commander of the king of Syria's army, brought to desperation by the loathed leprosy, is made a true believer and declares, "Indeed, now I know that there is no God in all the earth, except in Israel" (2 Kings 5:15). Circumstances that could have bred despondency and hostility in the little girl instead were powerless against her established good character.

Children I Have Come Across

There was a girl in my third grade Bible class one year who planned to memorize an entire chapter of the Bible. However, the weeks went by and she hadn't asked to recite any of it for me. Then, all of a sudden, she came to class ready to rattle off several lines or so. She saw my surprise and explained, "My dad said he was going to help me, but he never did. So I just did it myself." It would have been tempting to abandon the goal and blame it on her father, but she resisted this. Instead she took back ownership of her plan and proceeded without help. She did finally tackle that whole chapter—on her own. I admire her mettle.

There was a little boy in my Bible class years ago whose love of learning I have never seen rivaled among my students. He was fully engaged each class period, and I could see on his face the mental calculations he was going through to answer questions I posed. Many students dread having to commit scripture to memory, but not him. I would assign a new memory verse and tell him that when he memorized that one, I would give him another, framing it as a reward. In the next class period, he would just glow as he recited the memory verse and then smile from ear to ear when I chose another verse for him to take on. He was making God's will his own will by branding his memory with scripture. Last I heard, he was working on his PhD.

On one occasion I was duly impressed by the way a high school girl took over in a pinch. Late on Saturday night, we found out we were short a teacher in a children's Bible class for the next morning. One of the teachers in the class was out of town and trying to text several people to get a replacement. It was so late that no one responded. The teacher finally tried one of the high school girls early Sunday morning. The girl stepped in without hesitation and served in class as an aide to a child with learning disabilities, something not everyone can do. Did I mention that this teenager had also filled in that morning to prepare the communion?

There was a little girl, a fourth grader, in the 1960s who did not attend church. Her parents were not Christians. An elderly Christian couple in the neighborhood took a chance and asked her parents if they could bring their daughter to church with them. The child wanted to go, and her parents gave their permission. The little girl consistently got up and ready for services all by herself and would be waiting on the people to pick her up. Years later, as an adult, she explained that she took this privilege and the couple's favor very seriously and did not want to miss church services. My friend has been a very faithful Christian ever since.

William's Vision

William Estes, introduced in chapter 2, is the boy who suffers from amblyopia, or "lazy eye," in his left eye. His eyesight has improved, and so has his vision toward the future. For almost two years as part of his therapy, he has worn an eye patch over his good eye and had the vision in that eye blurred with eye drops to force his lazy eye to work harder. William's eyesight has improved from 20/200 (legally blind) in the left eye to 20/80 or better now.

Although the therapy brings no more improvement after the age of nine for most children, William, with God's provision, has beaten the odds. His eyesight has continued to improve until almost age ten. His parents, Julie and Tim Estes, expected for the regimen to be stopped by William's doctor when he turned nine, but the doctor announced that therapy would continue for another year. This turned out to be a tidy little test.

The doctor's orders were good news for his eyesight but bad news for a young boy who has been enduring near blindness, discomfort, and self-consciousness. However, when Julie told William that he had to hang on for another twelve months, he took it with the grace and maturity that he has been developing over the past two years.

Further, William has adopted a winner's frame of mind without enjoying the successes that keep most achievers motivated. From the beginning he didn't realize his vision was impaired, and the improvement since has been imperceptible to him. He feels no reward for all of the heartache. William has learned to do what needs to be done without expecting a reward.

Julie says, "He has become a pro at accepting that he has to take a few extra steps to meet everyone else at the finish line. But during it all he has happiness and hope." This is the embodiment of the term "grit" as developed throughout this book.

William's brother, Phillip, has also advanced in unexpected ways. Although he is technically the younger twin, Phillip looks after William and makes concessions to see that William is successful, safe, and comfortable. For instance, he watches out for William when walking through parking lots, as an older brother would. He knows when to leave the room if William needs extra attention from their parents. Phillip even comforts his mom when he sees she is struggling with the burden. He completes his household chores and helps William with his tasks—no prompting.

Julie says, "A part of [William's] prayer every night is for God to make his eye better. Then his brother prays for the same thing. They ask us occasionally if God has made it better yet. We always tell them

He is making it better and better all the time. I cannot wait until I can tell him he is done and God has won this battle for him." It will be added to the many key skirmishes that have already been laid to rest.

Haley

What makes good kids stand out? When I think about the kids I've taught who are outstanding from their peers, a common characteristic I recognize is their ability to be attentive. They listen, participate, and absorb in class. This is not something they can do simply because they were born with good genes. Rather, someone trained their brains to be able to pay attention. If concentration and mindfulness can be taught, there's every reason to believe your kids can get better at it. The stronger they are at paying attention, the easier it will be for them to learn, the better they will be at communicating, and the more clearly they will be able to think about important subjects like those we find in God's word.

It is tempting for parents to make excuses for the poor academic performance of their students, lamenting that they can't focus. I agree their children aren't concentrating, but perhaps the parents have not created an environment in which concentration was required. I recently went to a church service and sat behind a couple with a young child. This child was old enough to sit still but was not required to do so as the parents instead labored to satisfy his requests. It went this way: the mother gave a toy truck to the boy, who spun the wheels for twenty seconds, put it down, and outstretched his hand for something else. His mom rummaged through a bag to get him another toy. The cycle continued for the length of a sermon.

You may have seen a similar scenario play out, and there are so many things to note about the plot. First, while the parents' noble goal is to keep their son quiet and occupied during a church service, their tactics teach him that his role is to press them to provide entertainment for him. This early reinforcement may correlate to tough parenting that will be required when he is a teenager. Second, in the brief encounter with this family, it appears that this child is not taught to be attentive to anything but to succumb to all the sensory stimuli that trigger his brain. We can all identify with this attraction. We have information coming into our brains from each of our senses at every moment, and if a child learns it is acceptable to follow each trigger, his or her brain will never settle down.

God designed our nervous systems, so He innovated exactly how they work. He knows that we can easily become distracted and lose our attention, so He gave us a very practical way to overcome this—meditation. Many times in the Bible, we are told to meditate on things; what wisdom that is. In Psalm 4:4, David writes, "Meditate within your heart on your bed, and be still." He is instructing himself and his readers to do this to relieve distress and calm the mind.

In the New Testament, Paul writes to Timothy to "be an example to the believers in word, in conduct, in love, in spirit, in faith, in purity. Till I come, give attention to reading, to exhortation, to doctrine" (1 Timothy 4:12–13). Key to these directions is Paul's further guidance to Timothy: "Meditate on these things; give yourself entirely to them, that your progress may be evident to all" (4:15). Even someone young like Timothy should meditate, and no one will fail to recognize the maturity.

However, meditation, though a very simple thing, is extremely difficult for many people to do and requires practice. Teach your kids to meditate when they are young, and they will reap the benefits of being determined and becoming thoughtful and wise by using their own minds. If you're anything like me, you can benefit from teaching yourself too.

Meditation involves holding attention on a specific thought or idea for a period of time. Try it. Every time you find your mind wandering from this thought, bring it back to attention. When you first start, you'll find yourself constantly drifting. With training, you'll recognize more quickly when you're losing concentration, and eventually you'll be able to maintain intentness very well. Start by meditating for one minute, and as you improve, increase the length of the exercise. Have your children practice meditating and teach them not to react to every itch, sound, or smell. A child who can hold mental focus will be a better learner and wise beyond her years—worthy of another toast to success.

Rosalind

For Kids: Practical Tips on How to Become a Christian Success Story

Since we are free to make our own moral decisions, much of our level of success depends on self-starting, and that goes for children, too. The following is a list to help children begin to make their own strategies for the Christian life:

Participate

- Romans 12:4–8 tells us about how there are many members (Christians) of the body of Christ and that we all have different gifts and talents to use to help the body as a whole to grow. The writer argues, "if prophecy, let us prophesy in proportion to our faith; or ministry, let us use it in our ministering; he who teaches, in teaching; he who exhorts, in exhortation; he who gives, with liberality; he who leads, with diligence; he who shows mercy, with cheerfulness" (v. 6–8). Some kids are great at talking to others and joining them in. Some are good at taking care of Christians in need. Spend time thinking about what your strengths are and put these to good use. Write them down and recall them every day. If you have trouble pinpointing what you are good at, ask your parents; they will know. Never believe that you are too young to be useful to the church. In 1 Timothy 4:12, Paul tells Timothy not to let anyone discourage him because of his young age but that he should be an example—and you can be too.

Prepare

- If you are part of a Bible class, or any Bible study, always be prepared. Memorize your verses. Do the lessons your teacher assigns. Learning is so much more rewarding when you come prepared. Do you skip homework assignments at school? I hope not. The Bible lessons you are learning are even more important than what you are learning at school. Be grateful for your teachers' efforts in helping you understand. When they ask questions in class, participate in the discussion. Make sure you tell your teachers "thank you." From what I have seen, students rarely express gratitude to their teachers. You be the standout.

Share

- Jesus tells us, "Go into all the world and preach the gospel to every creature" (Mark 16:15), and that command includes you. Talk to your friends about what you are learning in Bible class, and invite them to come with you next time. Do you want to convert your family members, friends, and many more to Christ? Treasure your faith and be able to say, "I am not ashamed of the gospel of Christ" (Romans 1:16).

Not Just Sundays

- Remember that living the way God determines does not just apply when you are at church or with Christian friends. Put what you learn into practice everywhere you go. All that He commands should be part of the way you operate each day at school, sports and music practice, club meetings, and with your family at home—even with your siblings. They're also the neighbors God commands us to love.

Pray

- If you want to have your own success story, pray to God about it. Do you want to be a problem solver and a peacemaker? Ask Him to help you learn and grow and become a faithful follower of His—an effective worker. He can remake you in ways you never dreamed of, because He "is able to do exceedingly abundantly above all that we ask or think" (Ephesians 3:20). Asking is easy to do; it's also easy to forget to do.

Claire

Ever had a boss who never gave a "toast to your success" despite your going above and beyond? It can seem that way to children, too, when adults fail to acknowledge their spiritual steps forward. There are unlimited ways the world tells children and adults they should not be engaged in spiritual activities or fails to appreciate righteous behavior. This is why it is up to parents and other adults to encourage children to do the right thing—and then be diligent to acknowledge their success when they flourish.

It is unfortunate that not every single godly child becomes a godly adult. We can't take it for granted that our obedient young children will automatically follow God's call when they grow up. But resources are available to help us build a foundation that won't fail when life becomes more complicated and worldly enticements pull like an undertow.

I'm trying to get better at asking older people for observations and advice that will help me. Experienced parents can warn us about how to avoid pitfalls and bring children to the most favorable outcomes. We should praise and encourage Christians who have maintained their faith into adulthood. And chances are, a blessing for the ones we seek advice from will be their realization and celebration of a job well done in their own lives.

Some think of God as someone looking down on us as people who keep failing Him, never quite living up to His expectations. While we do fail, the truth is that God can also be happy with our service to Him. In 1 Kings 3:10, we see that God is pleased with Solomon in his pursuit of godly wisdom. That's right, God is pleased. He can be pleased with you and me, and we can find peace and happiness in that. When we reach our big and small goals in enriching children spiritually, it's time to pause and understand that God is pleased with the work we have done.

Colleen

The Rechabites

In Jeremiah 35, there's a short story that makes a lengthy point about programming and launching the next generation, about steadfastness. The historical setting is just before Jerusalem's fall to the Babylonians. The city is under siege by King Nebuchadnezzar—desperate times for God's people. God is disgusted with Judah's hardheaded denial of His laws and directs a real-life scenario to drive home the truth of what's going on.

The prophet Jeremiah is to invite the descendants of Rechab to the temple and then offer them wine to drink. When this occurs, the Rechabites refuse, stating, "We will drink no wine, for Jonadab the son of Rechab, our father, commanded us, saying, 'You shall drink no wine, you nor your sons, forever'" (Jeremiah 35:6). It does not appear that Jonadab is present, pressuring compliance. Also, note that the men don't cite their distaste for wine, its power to intoxicate, or any reason other than their father's command. God praises and rewards the Rechabites for their adherence; He criticizes Judah and Jerusalem for their lack of it.

Jonadab was effective in getting his children to comprehend and embrace his rules to be their own. These rules were still fastened after he was gone and when his boys and girls became adults. The Rechabites are proof that we can program our sons and daughters and expect them to continually live up to God's expectations and ours when they are out from under our roof and when our generation has passed on. They will eventually follow their own trajectory. The times when we're preparing to become parents, then guiding little ones in the formative years, and then advising them to become adults are like the architecture and development that go into the systems and technologies heading for launch into space. These components and our kids will inevitably operate separately from the ones who programmed them. Will they soar high with precision, dodging debris and settling predicaments? Or the opposite?

Operation Burnt Frost

Some launches are to be watched with cheers and high spirits that continue long after; some launches are best kept to whispers. Back in 2006, while the world went about its business, a National Reconnaissance Office satellite named USA-193 was uneventfully launched from Vandenberg Air Force Base ("USA 193" 2020). However, controllers on the ground lost contact with it. This enormous bucket containing one thousand pounds of very toxic hydrazine fuel was left to its own schemes in orbit, posing a risk to human life if it should slam into the earth (Steinhauser 2008). In early 2008 President George W. Bush ordered that the satellite be mitigated, initiating Operation Burnt Frost, the code name for the mission. The timeline for devising a plan to take it out was a matter of mere months. Following that there was an eight-day window of time to precisely target and intercept the off-track satellite (Garamone 2008).

After much planning and strategy, in February 2008 a Standard Missile-3 was launched and destroyed USA-193 in orbit. My research brought no definitive answers as to why USA-193 became a loose cannon, but I do know that twenty-four federal agencies made up of the world's greatest rocket science brains had to be rushed in to render it powerless to do damage.

Still on Duty

On the other hand, some launches go smoothly, with the ensuing mission continuing so loyally that we might completely forget about them. My friend and brother in Christ, Kevin Pierce, spent seventeen years in software development for the International Space Station (ISS) (Pierce 2019). The Space Station taunts the harsh conditions of space and provides a tolerable home for humans so that they can carry on research that fixes real-Earth difficulties.

Kevin sounds like a proud father when he says, "Every day, without failure, millions of lines of software code manage every aspect of ISS operation." This includes control and navigation of the orbiting vehicle and also basic functions we take for granted, like generating oxygen and clean water. "It was not perfect in the beginning, but like the ISS itself, it has evolved and improved to be one of the most complex and reliable systems ever developed," Kevin observes. This all clicks along while we go about our daily lives and pillow our heads at night.

Kevin sleeps well, too, because his "baby" is moving on without his help and certainly without the need to call in the emergency team to shoot something down. He cites four common and unfailing tenets held by his team of programmers that made them noteworthy and accomplished:

- A driving motivation to do the right thing.
- A commitment to the long haul.
- An abiding concern for each other and the collective good of the team.
- A sense of "mission" and an acceptance of team success first, individual success second.

For those of us getting the next group of godly people ready for send-off, there are plenty of ideas in his tenets to equip us for success. The ISS code was entered and developed properly at the start, and it can be the same with training children. Are there ever anomalies? Yes, but chances are that what you teach your young ones in childhood about committing to and knowing God will stick, especially if you follow through. It is not just getting them ready for the challenging—although expected—events of life but also guaranteeing that our younger people have the toughness to steer through whatever life hurls, hanging on with faith intact and heaven in unwavering sight.

Assignments

1. Back in chapter 2, about having a strong backbone, the assignment was to develop a new habit that takes self-discipline and requires that you follow through indefinitely. Discuss the new habit you began and describe your progress. Did you follow through? If so, what are specific ways that this has improved your self-discipline? If you did not follow through, analyze why. Then pick up the new habit again and continue where you left off. It is worth trying until you succeed.
2. Recite Luke 4:1–14 out loud from memory. You should have it memorized perfectly by now, but keep reinforcing it so that it will stay solid in your mind for the long term.

Chapter 12 Discussion Questions

1. There can be no doubt about the gratefulness that Tim and Julie Estes are experiencing with their son, William, as he has matured and developed his own resolve over the time of his treatment. William is still very young. In what ways will this process become more important, looking forward to his future? What effect has this journey had on his brother, Phillip?
2. Have you ever come across a child (your own or someone else's) who loved learning? What are some of the achievements you witnessed? How did you feel about your part in his or her successes? Did it make you want to help other students work harder to perform to their highest abilities? What was the result? In your opinion, what motivates some kids to self-discipline?
3. At what age should parents begin training their child's brain to be able to pay attention? Do you personally have the ability to concentrate so that you can teach your child to be attentive? State reasons it is important to learn the benefits of meditating. Haley gives some very relevant points on learning

the art of meditation. How can this exercise help your child to become a better learner?

4. Review the Practical Tips for Kids from Rosalind. This is excellent advice. Do you instill these gems of wisdom in your kids? At what age should this instruction begin? Some kids develop special strengths at a very early age. What would you do to encourage them to adopt these tips to become Christian success stories?
5. Have you ever referred your child to an older person or another Christian who would be better able than you to advise on a particular problem? Claire discusses the value of seeking guidance from other Christian parents who can share victories as well as mistakes made. What can parents learn from this sharing of information? What can your child learn?
6. As children become adults, it is inevitable that they will operate separately from the ones who "programmed" them. Our desire, as parents, is that they will soar high with precision, dodging debris and settling predicaments. In the section "Still on Duty," four common and unfailing tenets are listed to equip us for success in getting the next group of godly people ready for send-off.

   Discuss these points and tell how they can apply to teaching about committing to and knowing God. The goal is to get our children ready for the challenges of whatever life pitches and to hang on—faith intact. How will these help, in view of our desire that not only our children are committed to God, but also our children's children, and on and on?

For Personal Use

Write down the most important concept you gained from chapter 12 in regard to developing spiritual grit in families. Now personally review your answers for each chapter. What did you learn about yourself? What can you pass on to the next generation? Hopefully, this will have been a profitable study for you.

ABOUT THE AUTHORS

Colleen O'Steen has been a Christian for more than thirty-six years, having taught Bible class for nearly all of that time. She recently published *From Will to Power*, a book on spiritual self-discipline, and also performed the audiobook version. She has been a speaker at the Atlanta Women's Weekend and at the Truth Lectures. She is an adult and children's Bible class teacher and coordinator and has designed teaching materials, including the board game *Apostles in Action*, and multimedia presentations for the classroom covering the New Testament.

O'Steen is a professional writer, having worked in game, animated film, and virtual reality development; in promotion and marketing in the software industry; as a narrator; and as a television news anchor and reporter. She received a graduate certificate in instructional design from George Washington University, a master's degree in English from the University of Alabama in Huntsville, and a bachelor's degree in communication from the University of Alabama in Tuscaloosa.

Haley O'Steen, PhD, has been a Christian for more than thirteen years and has taught children's Bible classes. She is a finance professor. She earned her doctoral degree in finance from the University of Georgia, her master's degree in economics from Clemson University, and her bachelor's degree in economics and finance from the University of Alabama in Tuscaloosa.

Rosalind O'Steen Fort has been a Christian for more than thirteen years and has taught children's Bible classes. She is a commercial real estate mortgage underwriter. She earned her master of business administration degree from Florida State University and her bachelor's degree in accounting from the University of Alabama in Tuscaloosa.

Claire O'Steen has been a Christian for more than thirteen years and has taught children's Bible classes. She is a strategic proposals analyst. She earned her master's degree in global supply chain management from the University of Tennessee, studying in Germany and China. She earned her bachelor's degree in operations management from the University of Alabama in Tuscaloosa.

BIBLIOGRAPHY

Bowman, Dee. *The Joy of Growing Old in Christ.* Lakeland: Harwell/Lewis Publishing Company, 2019.

Cook, Shirley. Personal interview by the author. December 12, 2018.

Estes, Julie. Personal interview by the author. January 4, 2019, and January 31, 2019.

Fritzell, James, and Everett Greenbaum. *The Andy Griffith Show: The Best of Collection.* "Barney's First Car." Directed by Bob Sweeney. Fort Mill: United American Video (VHS), 1999.

Garamone, Jim. "Navy to Shoot Down Malfunctioning Satellite." United States Department of Defense, February 14, 2008, https://archive.defense.gov/news/newsarticle.aspx?id=48974.

Krumel, Jim. "St. Rita's First to Successfully Treat Rabies." *The Lima News,* posted February 17, 2018, limaohio.com/features/health/286238/st-ritas-first-to-successfully-treat-rabies.

Kuykendall, Ken. Personal interview by the author. December 13, 2018.

Petry, Nancy et. al. "2014: An International Consensus for Assessing Internet Gaming Disorder Using the New DSM-5 Approach." *Addiction* 109, no. 9 (2014): 1399–406.

Pierce, Kevin. Personal interview by the author. August 21, 2019.

Reed, Casey. "The Seabees at 75." Naval History and Heritage Command, May 10, 2019, history.navy.mil/content/history/nhhc/browse-by-topic/wars-conflicts-and-operations/world-war-ii/1942/building/Seabees-at-75.html.

Rousseau, Jean-Jacques. *Emile.* Mineola: Dover Publications, 2013.

"Seabee History: Formation of the Seabees and World War II." Naval History and Heritage Command, April 16, 2015, https://www.history.navy.mil/research/library/online-reading-room/title-list-alphabetically/s/seabee-history0/world-war-ii.html.

Steinhauser, Lucas, and Scott Thon. "Operation Burnt Frost: The Power of Social Networks." Appel Knowledge Services, June 1, 2008, https://appel.nasa.gov/2008/06/01/operation-burnt-frost-the-power-of-social-networks/.

Sunstein, Cass, and Richard Thaler. *Nudge: Improving Decisions Using the Architecture of Choice.* New Haven: Yale University Press, 2008.

"USA 193." National Aeronautics and Space Administration, Version 5.1.2, United States Government, May 14, 2020, https://nssdc.gsfc.nasa.gov/nmc/spacecraft/display.action?id=2006-057A.

Watts, Steve. Personal interview by the author. December 3, 2018.

Ziehlke, Austin. "52 Days to Life." Working paper. January 1, 2019.

Made in the USA
Monee, IL
07 November 2020